T0162831

Letters to Ellie

Grandma Bea Goode

iUniverse LLC
Bloomington

LETTERS TO ELLIE

Illustrated by Cindy Matikainen

iUniverse books may be ordered through booksellers or by contacting:

iUniverse LLC
1663 Liberty Drive
Bloomington, IN 47403
www.iuniverse.com
1-800-Authors (1-800-288-4677)

ISBN: 978-1-4917-1545-1 (sc)
ISBN: 978-1-4917-1546-8 (hc)
ISBN: 978-1-4917-1547-5 (e)

Library of Congress Control Number: 2013921279

Printed in the United States of America.

iUniverse rev. date: 12/5/2013

To Elliott Jane Kingsley.

If I could, I would give you the moon and the sun and stars at night. My wish for you has always been that you would grow up feeling the peace, love, and hope that you have filled my life with.

In my life, I have learned many things, but the most valuable lesson I've carried with me is that sometimes you need to just let it be. As I grow and learn from you, you continually teach me how to relax and enjoy the simple things that surround me at any given moment. Thank you so much for this.

The second most valuable lesson you continue to teach me is to try new things. One of my favourite books, which has touched my heart, is a book by Dr. Seuss called *Oh, the Places You'll Go!* It is my hope that as life changes you, you will have the courage to try new things knowing that you can conquer mountains with the exact same zest you had when you were young and I was watching you.

As you grow older, honey, know that you are loved. If you ever doubt how much you are loved, I hope you can find the time to read this book. It was written for you.

So take care, little honey. Live well. Take risks. Enjoy life and remember that you are loved.

Grandma Bea Goode

Contents

Acknowledgments

I was so grateful for the opportunity to write this book. At a time when life was a little scary and a little lonely, God sent me an angel to watch over and care for. Thank you, Ellie. You are the joy and the inspiration behind these stories.

Thank you to my oldest daughter and son-in-law for your support and for sharing your girls with me. I could not have written these letters without you.

Thank you from the bottom of my heart to my youngest daughter and son-in-law, whose support and undying belief in me have raised me up many times and lifted my spirits beyond measure.

Last year, I thought my book of letters was completed until I met my incredible illustrator. Thank you, Cindy Matikainen, for the seventy-four illustrations you have contributed to this book. At times, you have made me laugh so hard it took my breath away. You bring light and life to everything you do. You made these letters come to life, and now they are even more fun. I can't tell you how grateful I am that you came into my life. You are amazing.

Thanks to Sandi Emdin, BFF (best friend forever), DTM (Distinguished Toastmaster), and ME (mentor extraordinaire.)

You have pushed me, shoved me sometimes, and made it possible for me to grow. Your love and support are so greatly appreciated.

Thank you to all of my friends at Toastmasters. What a unique and wonderful organization you are—full of positive, caring people paying it forward for those coming behind them. It always amazes me when I sit down to a meeting and leave feeling entertained, inspired, excited, and happy. It's wonderful to be challenged and to learn something new each time I attend. Basil Morrison, one of our most experienced Toastmasters and one who continues to inspire, once said, "if you get out of Toastmasters what you want to get out of Toastmasters, you will never get out of Toastmaster's."

I wish to thank Trinity United Church for encouraging me to read my letters at their Talent Nights and for all the love and support I have received over the years. Thank you especially, Kathy Dahmer, Pam Brown, Rod and Pat Sein, Gary and Lori Foy, Mike, Liz and Vanessa Chorkaway, Linda Pulliah, Evelyn Cole, Donna Linville, and Kate Gravelle. I love my church, and I want to thank all of you for encouraging me and supporting this project.

Thank you, Gisele Guenard and Colleen Klevin, authors who have been published before me and who have been so very kind and helpful when I needed information or encouragement.

Thank you for the "group sessions" ladies of the Soul Club (Sandi Emdin, Lynne Raven, Gina Kennedy, Kate Rutherford, Michelle Ricard, Anick Gervais, Sheetal Pundir, and Myrna Furlani) for believing in me.

Thanks to iUniverse for your help getting this little book off the ground.

And finally, thank you, the reader, for supporting this book and enjoying these stories that are so dear to my heart.

You have brains in your head.

You have feet in your shoes.

You can steer yourself

any direction you choose.

You're on your own. And you know what you know.

And YOU are the guy who'll decide where to go.

And will you succeed?

Yes! You will, indeed!

(98 and 3/4 percent guaranteed.)

KID, YOU'LL MOVE MOUNTAINS!

-Dr. Seuss, *Oh, The Places You'll Go!*

CHAPTER 1

In the Beginning

January 16, 2006

Hi Little Elliott Jane,

Did you know that I have never written in a journal before? But your mommy gave me this blank diary and suggested that I start writing in it. This is probably due to the fact that I am always saying, "I should write that down before I forget."

And so it begins...

This morning, Mommy phoned because she wasn't feeling well and you were being you—active and adventurous. You are nine months old today, and you are very busy. I donned my hat and coat and drove the twenty-minute car ride to your door.

There is a gate at the top of the stairs in the entranceway of your house. I was thrilled when you met me at the gate, smiling all over. I love those big toothless grins. As I picked you up we looked at each other and smiled with our eyes and our hearts... and my true day began.

We played all morning. You love it when I talk to you, so I sat you in your high chair as I made supper for Mommy and Daddy, and we talked. I told you all about the stew I was making, and you made gurgling sounds as though we were having a real conversation.

As the day wore on and nap time became imminent, I brought you to the living room and made a cozy place with pillows and a blanket. Together we lay down on the floor. I touched your hair and your face as I sang, "I love your eyes, I love your chin, I love your nose, I love your belly button." You breathed deeply, smoothed my hair, and started to hum. Pretty soon, we were both humming away, and I began thinking about how much I love my little Ellie cat as we both dozed off.

An hour later, you awoke and were raring to go. You are learning and developing so quickly it is hard to keep up. This week, you learned that

1. a stick is made to make noise on the xylophone or tabletops, armchairs, or bowls;

2. if you put the ball in the hole of the tree of your plastic tree house, it will make the circles go round and round as well as start the music; and

3. it is possible to sit upright and you no longer need to support yourself on one arm like the usual bathing beauty pose we've all grown to love so much.

For Christmas, I had given you a red truck with three designs on the hood. One design was a circle, one a triangle, and the third one was a square. Last week, you learned how to put the square into the square, the circle into the circle, etc. But how to open the hood of the truck with one hand and remove the plastic toy with the other hand? Well, that was a mystery. But today, it was like you were saying, "Voila! Are you watching me, Grandma?"

"Every second, honey, every second." Then you showed me how you can put the circle into the circle hole. We held our collective breaths as, with tremendous concentration, you slowly lifted the lid with one hand and, with the other hand, reached in and removed the circle. Oh, the joy! Clap, clap, clap! Ellie, you are so clever! You were so excited and so proud of yourself that we both burst out laughing.

I think you are amazing, Ellie, my pally, my little Ellie cat, and I love you, love you.

Grandma Bea Goode

CHAPTER 2

Crib Cats

January 18, 2006

Hi Little Ellie Cat,

Mommy called me today. She asked if I would come to your place for tea. I could watch over you while she finished painting the animals on your bedroom walls. Today she painted a mommy wolf for protection and a baby wolf for peace and serenity. She designed it so that they would stand together for lasting love and prosperity. I love the way Mommy paints. She becomes so thoughtful and focused. I couldn't wait to get there.

Again, you met me at the gate at the top of the stairs. You crawled as fast as you could to the gate. Then you hauled yourself up on the wooden slats, out popped your toothless grin, and my heart soared again!

We began playing with your toys in the living room, but you became curious and wanted to see what was happening in your bedroom. You flashed Mommy a smile as if to say, "Hi, Mommy, can I paint too?" Mommy and I looked at each other for no more than three seconds, and when we looked back we noticed a whole bunch of tiny fingerprints all over the fresh paint. Mommy burst out laughing as she began painting over the little finger marks. Just as your tiny finger reached out at a new section of fresh paint, I picked you up and threw you into your crib.

You loved hanging out in your crib today. You'd crawl from one end to the other and literally smack your face into your cougar, your favourite toy. You also loved your lions, and you would press your face into one lion and then the other. I became convinced you were part lion. "Do you want to get out of there now, honey?" Nooooo waaaay! You are having wayyyy too much fun. You crawled away from me, and I caught you and tickled you and made you laugh. Then you crawled to the opposite end, and I had to follow and grab you again. More tickles and more laughs. It took more than a little convincing to get you to come out of that crib.

As I was getting ready to go home, you came over to me and as a sign of affection (I think); you slurped my face and hair. This slurping stage is driving your mommy, a true germaphobe, crazy. (And rightfully so... prior to licking me, you had just come from licking your cat, Coco!) Mommy said, "I am going to be sick," but I feel honoured—slimed but honoured.

I am marked.

How I love you, Ellie cat, and how you make me laugh.

Grandma Bea Goode

CHAPTER 3

Drum, Drum, Drum

January 20, 2006

Hi Little Ellie,

Once again, my day began with you at your gate at the top of the stairs. Once again, you grinned without teeth as you pulled yourself up to your feet by holding on to the wooden slats. But this day was different. You pulled yourself up on the gate, let go of the wooden slats, and stood, hands free, for one full minute... you concentrating, me barely breathing. Clever baby!

Mommy and Daddy went snowboarding today, so you and I spent the whole day together. Big day! I had brought a set of drums and noisemakers with me. As part of the set, there is a little xylophone that looks like a bug with a little worm stick, which is a baton. There is an A shaker and a round shaker. There are two drumsticks that look like caterpillars.

Baby, you love to drum! We drummed all day! We drummed on the coffee table. We drummed on the floor. We drummed on the chairs.

Then we started drumming on the xylophone. I started by playing a few notes and then handing the stick to you. You were funny. You were so introspective. You plunked away, but the xylophone noise was muted. You tried again hitting the keys of the xylophone. Again the sound was muted. You looked at me, and then at the stick, and then back at me. Finally, you passed the stick to me. "Do it again," you seemed to say, "and then I will understand how to do it!" And you did! *Plunk. Plunk. Plunk.* We had fun. I loved those drums.

When Mommy and Daddy came home, Mommy showed me how you and she play ball. You and Mommy sat facing each other, legs apart. Mommy rolled the ball to you. Most of the time, you were able to catch the ball, and we all remarked on how clever you were. Then we would all clap. It was fun. You passed the ball back to Mommy, who then rolled it back to you. You were right into this game when you looked over at me and saw that I was just observing. We could not believe it! You caught the ball and then passed it on to me. I rolled it back to you, and you passed it back to Mommy. We were flabbergasted! You had us taking turns! Over and over again, we passed the ball. We all loved it. Wonderful, wonderful baby! Imagine being able to include three people in playtime.

My world is a lighter, more awesome place because you're in it, and I love you, love you.

Grandma Bea Goode

CHAPTER 4

Little Mountain Climber

February 1, 2006

Hi Ellie,

You came to visit me today. You love to play with the toys in my toy box. You especially like my cuddly, blue Cookie Monster. When you push his tummy, he gives a real belly laugh and says, "Oh, that's fun, that's fun!" You and I are both pretty taken with Cookie Monster this week.

But today, your favourite toy was my couch. You've learned how to crawl up on the couch, hold on at the top, dig in with your little toes, and pull yourself up until you've reached the pinnacle. Then you make a sound that seemed to announce, "I am the greatest climber. I could climb Everest if I had a mind to!" Once the crowing is over, you let go, bounce on to the cushion, and jump. This is usually followed by a squeal of joy! Today, in addition to your climbing, you added an additional move of putting your feet down into the spaces between the cushion seats. Up and down you went. Up. Down. Let go. Bounce. Jump. Shove your feet into the spaces. Up. Down. Let go. Bounce. You were making me dizzy and I told you so. This made you laugh hysterically, which made me laugh too.

Every week, you make a new discovery. This week you discovered that the lines in a book have something to say to you. Your current favourite book is Einstein's *Young Animals*. Usually, you have a hard time sitting still long enough for a full story, but today you seemed to realize the connection between books and reading. You couldn't get enough (even though I'd heard from Mommy that you made her read Einstein's *Young Animals* twelve times prior to coming to my house. She had tried to convince you to experience a different book, but you were having none of it.) It was like you were saying, "I get it! I get it! Keep going with this! It's amazing!"

Something happened while you were making singing noises. I put my hand over your mouth, and you made the *aw, aw, aw* sound. You stopped and stared at me. Then you put the back of your hand over your mouth and you made the *aw, aw, aw* sound yourself. You were literally beaming with pride and pleasure. "Look what I can do." What a clever baby you are.

How you fill this old heart with joy. Wonder and fun are part of my day again, and I feel so blessed.

How I love you, little Ellie, my Ellie cat.

Grandma Bea Goode

CHAPTER 5

And the Beat Goes On

February 11, 2006

Hi Little Ellie,

I had the opportunity to babysit you today! My goodness, you were fun. Drumming has now become your thing. You can drum for hours and not get tired of it. Move over, Charlie Watts!

Today, your favourite thing to bang on was your little plastic drum. But you also wacked away at the piano stool, the cupboard doors, the floor, and at any toy that was handy. You thumped on the xylophone, on the window ledge, and on the back of a chair. I swear I could actually hear a beat in there... but I am your grandmother.

You are so interesting and you enjoy having your own private time in a private area. I love to watch you guard your privacy. You have a little corner of the kitchen away from the busy hullabaloo, and you guard this area protectively. This is your space. We all seem to be aware that this space belongs to you, and we leave you alone to play there. You keep your area tidy by using a cloth, preferably a damp cloth, but you are not particular about this. You take your cloth and rub the walls, dust the corners, scrub the floor. Around and around you go. You are very serious and very preoccupied with your "work." I could say that you are a real chip off the old block, but no, my home rarely gets that kind of attention!

You learned something spectacular this week. It is the value of the "power point." You have discovered that if you point your little index finger at something, people will vie for your attention and everyone will want to explain to you what you are pointing at. Oh, you had us running in circles. Point, point, point went the finger. "Look, look, look, Mommy [or Daddy or I]." "That's a fish. That's a picture. That's a cat. Can you say fish? Can you say picture? Can you say cat?" What a circus! And we all loved it.

Your teeth were hurting today, so you were very affectionate and wanted to stay close to me. Poor pet. "Up, Gwandma, up. Down, Gwandma, down. Up, Gwandma, up." You climbed up my leg by digging your little toes into my skin. Yikes, those little toes can hurt. I was so wishing that I could make you feel better. I so wanted to comfort you. But you wanted to climb me like a tree. I decided to sit down thinking I would help you reach my upper branches. You were reluctant to sit on my knee. The only position that seemed comfortable to you was to lean away, one elbow pressing into my side so that no part of you (except your elbow) was touching any part of me. "This is the way I want it today, Grandma," you seemed to be saying. Okay, little honey, whatever you want. Then you stood up on my knee, grabbed my face, and pulled yourself up using my ears. You stood up and wrapped your arms around my head, and then you started to touch my hair. You leaned forward and rested your forehead against my forehead, and you stayed and stayed.

Peace. My cup did run over, and my heart is filled with love... for you, little Ellie, my little Ellie cat.

Love ya, honey.

Grandma Bea Goode

CHAPTER 6

My Home Is My Castle

February 11, 2006

Hi Little Ellie, My Little Ellie Cat,

This week Mommy had to have some tests done in the hospital, so Auntie Sarah and I got to babysit you.

We were both fascinated by your antics. Your passion is *still* drumming, and you have become the world's greatest drummer. But you have also taken up exploring and experimenting with new things. Auntie Sarah and I nearly had a panic attack when you discovered how to drink water from the cat's dish. "No, no, honey, you can't do that!"

We brought you to the bathroom to wash you up and to brush your teeth. What started out as fairly serious soon turned into something fun. We started splashing and playing. You got soaked and we had to change your clothes.

Then it was quiet time for you. This week's favourite toy is a small piece of cloth, suitable for babies. If you have a cloth in your hand, you are happy. You took your cloth to your favourite corner. (This week it is the wall in the dining room beside the dining room table.) You concentrated hard to see if you could find a mark on the floor or on the wall. You turned around and around until you found something that suited your fancy... and you rubbed. Then you turned around, found another mark, and you rubbed some more. This seems to be a quiet, peaceful practice for you as though, when you rub, you leave your special mark on this place, saying, "This is my castle, and while I'm here, I own it!"

Auntie Sarah was wondering when you would warm up to her. You took your time, but we knew she was a winner when you left your corner to go over and sit beside her as she was sorting clothes, cross-legged on the floor. You pulled yourself up on her legs. Up, up you went, until you were standing on her legs and pulling on her ears. Using her ears as leverage you pulled yourself up even higher until you had a good lick of her hair. "I have been slimed," laughed Auntie Sarah. "Does this mean I am accepted into the club?"

You, Auntie Sarah have been blessed, thinks this grandma.

You bring such joy into the world, honey.

Love ya, little Ellie, my little Ellie cat.

Grandma Bea Goode
PS. This week your two favourite things are Auntie Sarah...
and blueberries!

CHAPTER 7

Lost and Found

March 14, 2006

Hi Little Ellie, My Little Ellie Cat,

I babysat you today, and you were such fun. Today your big interest was buttons. You especially liked the buttons on your TV. You would crawl over to the TV and pull yourself up. Then you would point towards the on/off switch and wait. I would stop whatever I was doing and say, "No, no, no, little honey, don't turn the TV off." You would then press the switch. The TV would turn off, and you would run/crawl away. I would catch you as you fled the crime scene and we would laugh.

You are taking more and more steps this week. I was going to say "alone," but that is not really the case when we are together. You like to take steps holding on to my finger. You like to use me to balance you. So we play around and around the grandmother. And you are so proud!

The other game you love to play this week is "lose something, find something." I was going to try to put you to sleep by reading to you, but I became sleepier than you and proceeded to drop the book onto the floor. Out of bed you got. Your feet hit the floor, and you began diligently looking under the bed for the book. You were wide awake, and I could see that nap time was not going to happen. So off we went to the kitchen to make a little snack. While we were there, you found one of your favourite toys: a bunch of plastic spoons on a ring. You pushed the spoons under the sink and pretended to cry. Then you shoved your hand under the sink, grabbed the spoons, and laughed so hard I thought you would choke. You did this again and again. It was hilarious! Your laugh was so contagious that I began laughing too… and that made the game even more fun.

Finally, you started to show signs of needing a nap, and I got to do my favourite activity, which is to rock you in my arms while giving you a bottle. I sang to you and stroked your hair. When you are tired, and only when you are tired, you seem to love this. You fell asleep in my arms, and I was feeling such love and contentment that I didn't want to put you into your crib. But I did. And you slept for over an hour.

When you did wake up, you were bonkers. You played in your crib for a while as you still love to play with your stuffed lion and cougar... rolling on them, falling on them, crushing your face and doing somersaults on them. Eventually I got you out of the crib and you tried the same kind of stunts on your cats, but they *really* didn't like it, so they made themselves scarce.

You are still into licking things this week. You've been trying to lick your cats, the fridge, or the stove. I try not to laugh because you really shouldn't be licking cats, fridges, or stoves. But every time I say, "No, no, no, Ellie!" you look at me, point, and say, "Bad, bad, bad!"

Don't laugh! I think to myself. Then I pick you up and try to distract you from the temptation of licking.

I am smiling as I write this. I get such a kick out of you. You make me laugh every day, and I thank God for the privilege of being around you.

Love ya, love ya, my little Ellie, my little Ellie cat.

Grandma Bea Goode

CHAPTER 8

Zowie, Owie, Owie

May 30, 2006

Hi Little Ellie,

You and your mom came to visit me today. Mommy came to help fix my window, so it was my job to play with you!

On the way into the house, one of the neighbours saw you outside and couldn't resist coming over to meet you. You were dressed all in pink today: pink capri pants, pink top with spaghetti string straps, and a pink hat. You looked so cute.

I had set up the shelves in my dining room because I knew you were coming. My house has a long row of shelves protecting the staircase, which leads to the basement. They are just the right height for a one-year-old. I had bought a gazillion little toys—tiny little dolls, Dora the Explorer, Sesame Street characters like Elmo and (your favourite) Zowie. I could hardly wait until you came over!

You were barely through the front door when you discovered the toy-filled shelves... and that was when my real day began!

"Hi, Ellie," I said.

"Hi, Gwandma." And then you yelled, "Zowie, Owie, Owie!" Before you stopped to explore the toys, you had to run! So away you went. First you visited the sunroom where there is a closet devoted almost completely to you. I have shelves in the closet stacked with toys, and you know that you are allowed to play with anything in there. You were excited and felt the need to run some more. So around and around the dining room table you went.

You discovered the step that goes from my dining room out into my little porch. This step is only about two inches high. Just your size. You practiced—up, down, up down, up, down, up, down. You were squealing with joy. Gosh, it was fun. Next you wanted to practice going up and down the stairs to the basement. Of course, you wanted to do this the way grown-ups do: one leg at a time. And of course, I can't let you do this by yourself, so I had my leg workout while you had the time of your life!

I have bead curtains in my basement separating my bedroom from the sitting room. You had a blast running through the curtains. "Look, Gwandma, I am Dora the Explorer!" You are such fun.

Finally, the window was fixed and we headed to a restaurant for supper. What an adventure. The restaurant had a fireplace in the middle of the dining area with a stage on either side. There were steps going up to the stage on each side. You *loved* this! Up the stairs you went, fast, one step at a time, and then down, fast, one step at a time, and then around the tables, and then back up the steps. The waitress left the room for a minute. As she went through the kitchen doors, you turned, raised your hands up as if to ask, "Where did she go?" and then you climbed back up on the stage. You stood there quite a while. You were listening to the music. You began to snap your fingers with your right hand, tap with your right foot, and bop your head up and down. You were really feeling the music. You stole the show! The customers loved it. Hey, baby, your very first performance!

Love ya, honey.

Grandma Bea Goode

CHAPTER 9

The Water-Skier

August 9, 2006

Hi Little Ellie,

Auntie Sarah had been out of town for a couple of months, and she and I couldn't wait to see you today.

When we first came to your house, you had just woken up, so you needed a little cuddle time with Grandma. You came wide awake though when you realized *Dora the Explorer* was playing on the television. "Dora, Dora, Dora!" you began to chant. We sang along with the TV. Auntie Sarah got a kick out of you as you waited, excitedly, for the part where Dora and Boots the Monkey clap along to the song. When Dora was over, you grabbed Auntie Sarah by the hand and helped her to load Zowie, your favourite doll, into the doll stroller. Hand in hand, you, Zowie, and Auntie Sarah strolled leisurely from the living room into the bedroom and back. Soon you wanted to make the game a little more exciting, so you let go of Auntie Sarah's hand and started to run fast, laughing and screaming, "Zowie, Owie, Owie!" as you went.

It's fun watching how you interact with people now. Auntie Sarah had brought you a book. As you started to look at the pictures, she asked you, "Can you find the kitten, Ellie?" And you'd point to the kitten. "Can you find the flower, Ellie?" And you'd point to the flower. Smart baby!

Auntie Sarah and I decided to take you for a walk. Joke. You took us for a walk! You would not hold on to our hands except for a jump. "I am going on my own," you seemed to say... down the middle of the ditch. You become fascinated with the dandelions in the ditch, with the tar on the road, and the ants on the sidewalk. We all had to stop and investigate these treasures.

Finally we returned home to play on the deck. Auntie Sarah and I had to work hard at getting you to be kinder to your cats, Coco and Beans. Mom has a water cooler on the deck for the cats... and you love it. You stuck your hand in the dish, wiggled your fingers in the water, and flicked the water into Coco's face. Then before Auntie Sarah or I could stop you, you grabbed Coco by one ear and started hauling her over to the water cooler! I know you think she could get a better drink there, but you are not so gentle, baby. Coco ran behind the swing for safety.

Last week, your mommy was really worried because you had started water-skiing behind the cats—both Coco and Beans. You would hold onto the cat's tail, and they would take off trying to get away from you. You would hold on, screaming with glee, while the cat pulled you across the hardwood floor. "Oh my goodness! Stop! Stop!" Mommy screamed. And of course, you stopped. But what a sight you were as you flew across the room. You, Coco, and Beans were given a time-out, and Mommy had to help you make amends. I think they have both forgiven you... or at least one of them has. Perhaps you will be a little more thoughtful about using their tails as the rope behind your motorboat... but I'm not sure!

As well as being mischievous, you have an incredible sense of humour and fun. For example today, after your nap, I said, "You don't need that soother now that you're awake, Ellie. So give me the soother, okay, honey?"

"Okay," you said. You took the soother out of your mouth and started to hand it to me. Then with a twinkle in your eye, you snatched the soother back and plopped it back into your mouth. You clamped your little gums of steel around it and then you burst out laughing. How you light up my life.

How I love you, my little Ellie cat.

Grandma Bea Goode

CHAPTER 10

Hide That Tattoo

August 16, 2006

Hi Little Ellie,

We babysat you today, Auntie Sarah and I. This is your shy period, so at first you would have nothing to do with Auntie Sarah, but it didn't take you long before you were doing your little tap dance around her. Your current hairstyle consists of two little ponytails that stick straight up off your head. You looked so cute as you jitterbugged around Auntie Sarah, knees high, ponytails jiggling in the air. Auntie Sarah sat on the floor with a little Tonka toy truck, and on each bypass, she ran the truck over your foot and partway up your leg. You thought this game was the *best* and you played "circle Auntie Sarah" again and again.

On one of your bypasses, you discovered that Auntie Sarah had a tattoo on her back. The tattoo is an intricately designed lotus flower with flames in the center and around the outer edges. Auntie Sarah believes that lotus flowers are a symbol of peace and love and that they bring her luck. On one of your bypasses you stopped at Auntie Sarah's back, knelt down, yanked her shirt up, and had a really good look at the lotus flower. "Hi!" you exclaimed. You touched the lotus leaf and made a face. Then you pulled Auntie Sarah's shirt down hard, and you shook your head. No, no, no, we are not going to be looking at that tattoo again.

Then you took Auntie Sarah by the finger—"Come." You brought her downstairs and introduced her to your play castle. Your castle has a bridge and a moat with a slide. You indicated that Auntie Sarah was to go inside the castle. Then you walked to the bottom of the basement stairs and yelled, "Gwandma, Gwandma, come!" We met at the bottom of the stairs, and you took me by the finger, led me over to your castle, and began trying to convince me to get inside. But I just wouldn't fit in there, and you soon realized that there was no way you were going to be able to stuff me inside that thing. It was not easy for you, but eventually you gave in, grabbed me by the finger again, and indicated that instead of stuffing me into your castle, you were going to let me help you play on your slide. Holding onto my finger, you climbed up the incline and slid down the slide—fast! You laughed and ran around. Then you grabbed both my hands and climbed up the slide. You then jumped off the bridge into Auntie Sarah's arms. She threw you high in the air, twirled you around, and set you back down on the bridge. With your head tilted back, you laughed so hard that it made us laugh too. We did this again and again, until Auntie Sarah and I were so tired that we couldn't do it anymore.

It was then time for a nap, and Auntie Sarah offered to put you down. She read you stories as you played with her hair. Soon your eyes crossed and the hair twirling slowed down. You were asleep.

I know in my grateful book I will talk about the tattoo and your reaction to it... and how you ran in circles around Auntie Sarah. But the absolute best part of my day was when you called for Grandma from the bottom of the stairs.

You are always in my grateful book, little honey.

You are the fun in my life, the light and the joy, and I love you, love you.

Grandma Bea Goode

CHAPTER 11

Cereal Mania

August 18, 2006

Hi Ellie, My Little Ellie Cat,

Auntie Sarah and I visited you again today. What an adventure. We had to go out and do a little bit of shopping, so we decided to stop at Swiss Chalet for lunch. You were so good. You loved sitting in the special chair they had brought over for you. You were interested in everything and everybody. When you did start to fidget, Auntie Sarah distracted you by singing, "One, two, buckle my..." You would sing, "Shoe!" And we would all clap. Then Auntie Sarah would sing, "Three, four, shut the..." And you would sing, "Door!" And we would all clap again. Then, "Five, six, pick up..." "Sticks!" you scream. And we all clapped again. We were having so much fun that we were surprised when lunch arrived.

After lunch, we went to your house. You were a little ball of fire. We were hardly in the door when you grabbed Auntie Sarah by the finger and started to run into the bedroom, back through the living room, and into the kitchen. On one of your passes, you stopped and grabbed my finger too. And voila, we were all up and running. *This is a party!* I remember thinking.

Because it was a party, we decided to bring out the keyboard. At first you, Auntie Sarah, and I were dancing freestyle on our own. We were snapping our fingers, waving our arms in the air, turning in circles, and giggling. You then decided to beef things up, so you started dancing in circles around me. Then you stopped behind my back and started to giggle. You tapped me on the shoulder and twirled away next to Auntie Sarah. You stopped behind her back and tapped her on the shoulder. Soon we were all laughing and dancing and trying to catch the little leprechaun who kept tapping us on the shoulder. Where was that little trickster?

Some of us had to stop and rest. Auntie Sarah and I flopped down on the couch while you sauntered into the kitchen on your own. As Auntie Sarah received a phone call, I relaxed and closed my eyes. Auntie Sarah drifted into the kitchen to see what you were up to. I could hear a bit of scuffling around and then a plea, "Mom, Mom, come quick, I need you!" You, little Ellie, my pally, had upturned a whole box of ooey, gooey, sugar-coated honey nut cereal all over the kitchen floor. Then you discovered that the most fun a little girl could have would be to jump up and down, stomping on the cereal. Kicking seemed like a blast too. You were having a ball. There was cereal everywhere. Auntie Sarah was trying to hold you so you wouldn't run through the cereal. She was trying to continue her conversation on the phone at the same time. You, of course, wanted down. You won!

All of a sudden the cats got involved. Auntie Sarah and I were trying desperately to get things cleaned up, but every time we started to make a little headway, another pile of cereal would go flying. The cats were jumping and chasing the cereal; you were giggling and throwing cereal at the cats. You and the cats seemed to think that this was the best game ever invented. I watched as the cereal flew around the room, the cats flew after the cereal, and you flew after the cats. I stopped. I looked at you. I looked at Auntie Sarah (who now looked horror-stricken), and I started to laugh. Auntie Sarah and I both sat down in the middle of the chaos and laughed like maniacs. You are such fun!

I was taking a moment to catch my breath after the kitchen had been returned to normal. You could finally see the floor. I was drinking some bottled water, and you decided that you wanted a drink of it too. I offered you your own little bottle of water. Then you started to tease me. You grabbed my bottle of water and began to shake it—"Look at me." You started to laugh and shook the bottle harder. It began to take on a rhythm—shake, shake, shake the bottle, laugh, shake, shake, shake the bottle, laugh. Then you dropped the bottle, which, thankfully, still had the lid securely in place. You ran over to me and threw your arms around my neck. My heart filled over with joy. I am so grateful for the fun you bring into my life. I will never forget today, and the video camera in my head will run this film again and again. Each time it does, it is sure to make me smile.

How I love you, little Ellie, my little Ellie cat.

Grandma Bea Goode

CHAPTER 12

Don't Entionmay the Airhay

August 11, 2006

Hi Little Ellie,

Auntie Sarah and I visited you again today. You were as excited to see us as we were to see you. We had fun sliding with you, on our behinds, down the slippery slope beside your house. Then you explained to us that you knew where to find some raspberries, and you led us right to them. The sun was shining, the air was sweet, and I swear those were the best-tasting raspberries I have ever eaten.

We had a great day playing in the sunshine, but soon it was time for bed. Bedtime is your hardest time. When you get tired, you get really cuddly and you want your mommy. But tonight, at bedtime, you were as energetic as the energizer bunny. Mommy decided to take a bath first while you hung out with Daddy, Auntie Sarah, and I. You picked up a Chinese food menu that had been left lying on the coffee table. You ran to the bathroom, gibbering the whole way. "Come on in, Ellie," said Mommy. You showed her the menu and pointed to the selections. "Hmmm, I'll have chicken balls with sweet and sour sauce," said Mommy. You ran back to Daddy, menu in hand. "Chatter, chatter, chatter, goo," you said. "I'll have chicken fried rice," he answered. You gibbered away again. Then you said okay. You took your menu back to Mommy. "Chatter, chatter, chatter, goo," you recited again. Mommy said, "I'll have chicken chow mein."

"Okay." Back to Dad.

"I'll have beef and vegetables." And on it went until you finally grew tired of the game.

Then you were on to your favourite pastime—running. You ran from the living room into the bedroom and back to the living room. You were so cute running as fast as you could, feet high in the air, ponytail standing up on top of your head. You put on quite a show, and we were loving it.

Auntie Sarah laughed when I said to Mommy, "Oh, look at Ellie's hair. I love the ponytail!" Mommy panicked and exclaimed, "Don't entionmay the airhay or the onytailpay! If you do, she'll take it out!" Sure enough, you immediately removed the elastic from the top of your head, running as fast as you could and giggling with glee as you went. How you make us laugh!

Soon it was time for Auntie Sarah and me to go home. We were quiet and introspective on the drive back to my house. I noticed Auntie Sarah smiling. She was a little wistful, and I think, knowing she has to leave again tomorrow, she was missing you already.

I close my eyes and relive the events of the day in my mind. I am so grateful to have spent the day with you and my girls and to be experiencing the beautiful memory of you running and skipping in the sunshine, my little sunshine girl, my beautiful Ellie of the Raspberries.

Love you, Ellie, my pally.

Grandma Bea Goode

CHAPTER 13

Just Taste Those Bubbles

October 4, 2006

Hi Little Elliott Jane, My Little Ellie Cat,

We had such fun today. You came to my house to play. As per usual, we had to wait for you to enjoy your favourite two-inch step from my porch to my dining room. So up, down, up, down, up, down you went. You still seem to love this game even after a few months, and we are not able to get you inside the house quickly.

Next you spotted my corn plant, which is just inside the door. I have two little clay animals who live in the dirt. I think they are lions, or maybe they are pigs; either way, I love them, and so do you. You knelt down, waved, and said, "Hi! Hi!"

After our clay animal meet and greet, we made our way into the sunroom, where I had left a big, black teddy bear waiting for you. You were very excited when you realized he was yours, and you immediately wanted to take him for a walk. So off we went. We stopped to admire my neighbour's flower bed, and you bent down to have a sniff of the pretty hydrangeas. Sniff, sniff, pluck! We smiled apologetically at my neighbour, and I thought perhaps we should try another activity besides flower sniffing!

Later, we went to your house for a girls' night with just you, Mommy, Auntie Sarah, and I. You were hungry. You kept dragging Auntie Sarah by the finger. "Come, come," you would say (because you had spotted the corn on the cob.) "Corn, corn!" you yelled. You wanted some *now*! But you know, baby, some things in life really do need to be cooked first—so we tried to distract you with carrots.

After supper, we played in the living room. You had gotten into the pots and pans and found a big red strainer that you promptly fell in love with. You went from one of us to the other. Each of us had to taste the imaginary spaghetti. Then you came to me. I was resting in the big chair. You took me by the finger and removed me from the chair. You said, "Gwandma!" You were very firm. Apparently the chair I had chosen was where the red strainer was supposed to be sitting, and it was the spot where he *was* going to sit. I had better find another seat because that seat was taken, by golly.

The night moved on, and Mommy poured you a bath with lots of bubbles. You loved it. You tried to flick the bubbles with your hand. You put your face in the water and tried to lick the bubbles. "Yuck!" you yelled. Mommy said, "Don't eat the bubbles then, honey." But you were interested in how the bubbles tasted, and so you tried licking them again and again. "Yuck, yuck!" is all we heard for a while.

When you were all finished we went to your bedroom, where Mommy tried to dress you for bed. But you were revitalized and did not want to be still. You called for me: "Gwandma! Come!" I thought you wanted a hug and I was beaming—but you wanted me to save you from your terrible mother who wanted to put pyjamas on you. It didn't work. So you hollered, "Sarah! Sarah! Come!" Auntie Sarah hugged you too. It was too much for a little girl who did not want to put her pyjamas on! You pushed Auntie Sarah away. Mommy explained to you that you can't push people because it may hurt their feelings. Then you smiled at Auntie Sarah and gave her a big hug. You called me back to your room knowing it was time for us to go home. You grabbed my finger and pulled me down onto the floor. We sat looking at each other for a few minutes. You didn't really want me to go. I was so honoured. I didn't really want to leave you either. Then we looked at each other. "Aren't we silly?" You smiled. I smiled.

Bye, bye, little love.

Grandma Bea Goode

CHAPTER 14

The Sweeper

November 29, 2006

Hi Little Ellie,

I took you to play school yesterday and you hated it. We stayed for about two minutes, and then we left. Mommy thought we should give it another try, and I thought so too. So we went back to play school today. This time you liked the toys and the big dollhouse. I knew we hit pay dirt when you discovered the wooden puzzles. I could hardly wait to get home so I could call Mommy and tell her how you were able to do the puzzles. You pulled out the hammer and put it back exactly where it was supposed to go. You pulled out the drill and put it back too. You were pretty proud of yourself. Things were going along really well until you wanted to explore outside the classroom.

Your eyes lit up when you discovered an empty hall. You love to shop, and when you shop, you love to run up and down the aisles until you can hardly stand up. The empty hall looked like a store, so, of course, you wanted to run down these halls too. You were very curious. You wanted to go into each and every classroom. How frustrating that I couldn't allow you. You were not a happy camper. Soon home started to look good to both of us.

When we got home, Daddy was waiting for us. You made him lie on the floor. You have a little blanket. It is about the size of a dish towel. You covered Daddy up and patted his head, saying, "Night, night." Later, once he was allowed to get up from his "nap," he tried to sweep the floor. But he had a little helper who loves to run through the dirt. You ran to the living room. "Gwandma, come. Dad sweep!" Then you laughed, ran to the kitchen, made a beeline for Daddy's dirt pile, and scattered it all over laughing and yelling the whole time. Daddy and I decided to forget the pile of dirt for the moment. You and I would deal with it later. He laughed and left for work. Eventually, we got the floor swept.

After our floor sweeping, you took me by the hand and brought me to your bedroom. Obviously, it was nap time. You climbed up on the bed and said, "Hairy." Hairy is your favourite stuffed animal. Then you said, "Book." So we found Hairy and your *There's a Wocket in my Pocket* book and settled in. It wasn't long before your eyes were crossing, as were mine, and I don't know who fell asleep first.

How I love you, my dirt-kicking angel.

Grandma Bea Goode

CHAPTER 15

Jewels in the Sun

January 7, 2007

Hello Little Ellie, My Pally,

I babysat you today. I brought with me the set of Dora dishes I had given you for Christmas. They are porcelain dishes to be used with supervision. Since our tea parties always consist of at least the two of us, this is never a problem. You love the dishes and you love tea parties. Today it was your turn to pour. I filled up the teapot and the cream and sugar bowls with juice. You poured tea from the teapot into the cups and then onto the saucers... and then we slurped. You laughed. I laughed! Then... I cleaned up apple juice from the floor, the table, and all the teeny, tiny dishes. Tea parties can be messy, but they're worth it!

It was a beautiful day. The sun was shining for a change. The trees were covered in a light dusting of snow, and it was cold, but not so cold that we couldn't go outside. So we bundled up and went for a walk. "Come see, Ellie! Isn't this pretty!" I said as we passed a tree whose branches were laden with snow. You repeated my words. "Come see," you said. We made snowballs and played kick the snowball and slid on the ice. What fun!

You didn't want to go back home yet. You wanted to climb to the top of the big hill just around the corner from your house. "It's a big climb," I said. "I can't carry you back. Are you sure you want to go up that big hill?" Oh yes, you were sure. We made it to the top of the hill, and we discovered a little bush covered in ice and glistening like a jewel in the sun. It looked so beautiful. But you, Ellie, my pally, were tired... too tired to walk back home! "Up, Gwandma, up!"

"Can you walk a little ways?" I asked as I tried to put you down. But you curled up your little feet. Those feet of yours were not going to go anywhere near that ground. This tired little grandma had to carry you all the way home giggling at my feeble attempts to try and get you to walk. Next time, we're going to bring a sleigh.

A walk in the snow should always be followed by hot chocolate. "Hot chaw ca lot!" you yelled. We must have it using your new tea set. This means another mess to clean up, but it is such fun to put our pinkie fingers in the air and sip our hot chaw ca lot!

Soon it was nap time and you were tired from being outside. You wanted to cuddle and so did I. I read you several stories and lay with you until you fell asleep.

I had the best day, honey. You can bet I went home with a smile on my face and in my heart.

How I love you, little Ellie, my jewel in the sun.

Grandma Bea Good

CHAPTER 16

The Shower

January 26, 2007

Hi Little Ellie Cat,

I went to your house today. I was so excited to see you. You were happy to see me too. We laughed and played. What fun you are! I made pasta and veggies for lunch (a package deal.) You hated it. "Yuck, yuck!" you said. So rice and peas it was... again.

You are really talking these days. I brought out some toys to play with: Scooby-Doo and Pinky (the teddy bear Aunt Tess had given you for Christmas). Pinky is pink plaid with a really neat old-fashioned hat and a boa fur scarf. You chose her name, which I thought was quite fitting. You brought Pinky over to your other toys. "This Pinky," you said while holding Pinky up in front of your other toys. Then you patted your chest and said, "Ellie." You pointed at me, "This… Gwandma." Then you picked up Scooby Doo and brought him over to the toys. "This Scooby Doo," you said. Again you pat your chest several times and said, "Me… Ellie." You pointed your finger at me. "This… Gwandma." The introductions were complete. I laughed much harder than you thought necessary because it reminded me of an old Tarzan and Jane movie.

You were really loving today, lots of hugs and lots of cuddles. I was enjoying the attention. We always love listening to music and dancing. I had brought my ghetto blaster, so we turned up the tunes and danced up a storm! What fun!

Mommy phoned me tonight to tell me about the shower. Daddy had gone to work, so Mommy had to bring you into the bathroom while she showered. She had explained how you must stay in the bathroom until she was finished. You thought this was pretty exciting. As soon as Mommy turned the water on in the shower stall, you opened the curtain. "Hi, Mumma!" And water poured out of the shower stall onto the bathroom floor. Mommy continued to shower, and then she heard a little noise that sounded like "wheeee!" You were sliding across the bathroom floor! Again you opened the curtains. "Hi, Mumma!" Again water poured out of the stall, onto the floor, and all over you. Mommy said you were completely soaked but having a ball. It became a game. You continued to skate from the shower stall to the bathroom door and back, opening the curtain and yelling, "Hi, Mumma!" each time. Finally, Mommy had to give up. She grabbed a towel, stepped and got out of the shower, removed all of your very wet clothes, and carried you into the shower stall for your very first shower. Mommy laughed as she told me how many towels it took to clean up the water.

Before going to bed, you asked Mommy, "Phone Gwandma, Mumma!" And you did. "Hi, Gwandma," you said.

"What did you do tonight, Ellie?" I asked.

"Took shower!" you yelled. "Ellie took shower!" Then you said, "Made big mess!" *Hmmm, I'll bet you did*, I think, smiling. Mommy prompted, "Helped clean up."

"Clean up," you said.

As usual, you didn't say good-bye, but according to Mommy, you waved at the phone. I am left feeling warm and fuzzy.

You are so amazing.

Love ya, honey!

Grandma Bea Goode

CHAPTER 17

The Shadow

January 28, 2007

Hi Little Ellie, My Pally,

You are such a little character, and you're really developing your sense of humour. You and Mommy phoned me tonight. You had just come out of your bath. Mommy said, "Time for a diaper." With a smile, you said to Mommy, "Time for *no* diaper." And you took off running to the kitchen. When you got there you found that the lights had been turned down and there were shadows on the floor. You became very interested in your own shadow, which seemed to be following you around. You started chasing your shadow to see if you could catch it. This was great fun! For a moment, you seemed to think your shadow was too big, so you tried pushing it back, to no avail. You were not about to give up, but it was bedtime, and you left feeling pretty frustrated with that pesky shadow.

See you tomorrow, little honey. My day has, again, ended with a smile... because of you.

You are the light of my life, and I love ya, love ya.

Grandma Bea Goode

CHAPTER 18

The Soap Bubble Story

February 6, 2007

Hi Little Ellie, My Pally,

We had so much fun today. We made shapes out of Play-Doh. I made snakes. Daddy made snowmen. You made balls.

You were talking a lot today, and the grown-ups were having such fun listening to you. When Mommy came home from work, you were very glad to see her, and you didn't want to leave her side. You greeted her with, "Hi, Mumma." Mommy said, "I have to go to the bedroom for a minute. Do you think you could wait here or do you want to come with me?" You said, "Come with me!" Mommy tried to explain, "Come with *you*." It sounded pretty confusing to me and it made me laugh.

You were hungry and started to cry. Mommy said, "You have to say the words, honey. Can you say 'I'm hungry'? Can you say that?" You said, "That!" We smiled and you had something to eat.

When bath time was nearing you said, "Tub me, Mumma, tub me!" I came in to see the bubbles. I sneezed loudly, and you thought this was the funniest thing that you had ever heard. What a belly laugh!

As Mommy left to take a phone call, you started to tease me. You picked up your favourite little bath doll, Hilary. She is 1 ½ inches tall with lots of curly hair, and right then she was full of soapsuds. You plunged Hilary into the soapy water, which sprayed all over me. It surprised me and I let out a little yelp. You stopped and looked at the water dripping all over me… and you laughed! You little rebel. You thought this was so funny! So you did it again and again. We were laughing so hard that Mommy came in to find out what going on. "What's happening in here?" she asked. Mommy looked at me with my dripping nose, my hair soaked, and my clothes covered with soapy water. At first I thought she might be a little upset, but she burst out laughing. Then you and I burst out laughing again. Gosh, you're fun.

Mommy told me you were teasing Daddy last night. Mommy would say, "Kiss Daddy good night." You would look at Daddy with a twinkle in your eye and then go over to your cat. You would kiss your cat Coco and say, "Good night Coco!" And then you would laugh! Mommy would say again, "Say good night to Daddy and give him a kiss." You would say, "Good night Coco" and kiss your cat. Then you would look at Mommy and Daddy again and again laughing. Soon, you, Mommy, and Daddy were all laughing and a whole little family had a fit of the giggles.

I made supper for us tonight. You often tease me by saying "Yuck!" But tonight I cooked corn on the cob. You like to be able to pick up the whole piece of corn. It makes me smile because my daughters tease me about getting corn on my face and in my hair when I eat corn on the cob. "Please, Mom," they say, "don't eat corn on the cob in public." And then they laugh. We all laughed tonight as both you and I enjoyed the corn. Corn, corn, we love corn. And Grandma loves you.

Good night, little honey.

Grandma Bea Goode

CHAPTER 19

Drifting Snowflakes

February 18, 2007

Hi Little Ellie, My Pally,

I babysat you today. As usual, we sang and danced all day long! We love the songs "The Wheels on the Bus" and "Polly Anna All the Day."

We played "chase the baby." You love to run. You put your right hand in the air or both hands behind you (which makes me very nervous.) You yell, "You can't catch me!" And the chase is on. Heaven forbid that Grandma should sit down for a minute. She should not!

You became fascinated with the plastic bag we use to store your Play-Doh. "Oop, Gwandma, oop!" You were very curious about what was inside that bag and seemed disappointed when you found out it was only Play-Doh.

You became quite distracted when I exclaimed, "Ohhhh, Ellie, look at the snowflakes. They're as big as cotton balls." With wonder in your voice, you repeated, "Snowflakes." You went to the front door and banged on it. "Oop, Gwandma, oop!" ("Oop" is your new word for "open.") We watched in awe as the soft, huge snowflakes came tumbling down. "Catch, Gwandma!" We tried to catch the snowflakes on our hands and on our tongues. Oh gosh, I hope Mommy or Daddy don't walk in and catch us with this door wide open trying to catch snowflakes when it is twenty degrees below zero! Sometimes you're a bad influence on me. We had to open the door and catch snowflakes three or four times before you were satisfied. They were fascinating, those snowflakes, as they danced and swirled in the sunlight.

You were very affectionate today. I received many hugs and kisses. At nap time, I had to read six fairy tales before you finally consented to closing your eyes and going to sleep. As I watched you sleeping, I wished, for you, visions of peaceful snowflakes drifting gently down, soothing you and filling your soul with as much joy as you bring to mine.

Love ya, little honey.

Grandma Bea Goode

CHAPTER 20

Tap, Tap, Tap, Says the Woodpecker

March 20, 2007

Hi Little Ellie, My Little Ellie Cat,

I'm thinking about you tonight. You, Mommy, and I went shopping last Saturday. You love to run in the store. You love to crawl behind the boxes on the bottom shelves—if you can find them. You also love balloons, especially when they are on the ceiling of the store.

Prior to shopping, you and Mommy made muffins. Mommy called to explain how you and she were supposed to be baking six muffins, but by the time you had stirred and tested the batter, she only had enough for five.

Mommy made honey oatmeal muffins. She stuffed chocolate chips inside. You would take a muffin, remove all the dough, and eat only the chocolate chips. Mommy said, "Ellie, you need to eat some of the muffin too, not just the chocolate."

"Mumma," you said, "Ellie likes chocolate!" You're a baby who knows what she likes.

You were talking so much this week. Your favourite sentence is, "What's that sound?" You say it fast and it sounds like, "Whassasound?" When you woke up on Saturday morning Mommy was lying beside you. "Mumma, Mumma, what's that sound?"

Mommy said, "I think that's a helicopter."

You responded, "No! Mumma, that's a truck on the road!" So okay, little honey, Mommy thinks you must be right.

Monday, when I was babysitting you, we went for a walk in the fresh snow. You love making paths in the snow. We crossed the street and were looking at the big evergreen tree on the other side of the road. We heard *tap, tap, tap, tap, tap!* "What's that sound, Gwandma?" you asked. "I think that's a woodpecker," I said. We moved closer to the tree and looked up. There he was, a woodpecker in the tree. Once again, he tap, tap, tap, tapped his beak into the wood. "Ellie," I whispered, "see the woodpecker, look, look!" You could see the woodpecker too. Oh, we were excited! We absolutely had to go back home for some celebratory hot chocolate.

At home I looked up the woodpecker in your bird book for you. But you weren't as interested anymore and were much more excited to dance and play games.

You didn't mention the woodpecker for the rest of the day, and I thought you had forgotten about him. But you could hardly wait for Mommy to come home from work, and I hadn't seen you this anxious in a long time. At last Mommy came home. "Hi, Ellie, how's my girl?" she asked. Immediately you said, "Woodpecker, Mumma, woodpecker!" I hadn't realized you had been waiting to tell her about the woodpecker all day! You and Mommy looked at the woodpecker in your bird book. Then you started jumping up and down. "Mumma, Mumma, call Dadda, call Dadda—woodpecker!" Mommy called Daddy at work. You could hardly wait for him to come on the line. "It takes a moment to find Dadda sometimes, Ellie. We have to give him a minute," said Mommy. Daddy finally got to the phone. You were so excited. "Woodpecker, Dadda. Woodpecker!" Daddy laughed and told you he loved you and then happily hung up the phone. We were all smiling as you hung up the phone.

What a wonderful, heart-warming moment for us all to share.

Love you, little woodpecker spotter.

Grandma Bea Goode

CHAPTER 21

Holding Hands

April 8, 2007

Hi Little Ellie,

I hosted Easter at my house this year. You arrived with Mommy and Daddy. Auntie Sarah and her friend Heung Ju were already here.

You love coming to my house and were excited the minute you stepped in the door. As usual, I had your little toys out at eye level for you. I had set out a big, black teddy bear and you loved it. You said your hellos to the little clay animals in my corn plant, which Auntie Sarah had given to me a long time ago. You are not the only one who loves the plant critters. You took a shine to Heung Ju, and she was immediately mesmerized by the joy you brought to the room.

You ran up and down the stairs, around and around the dining room table, laughing, giggling, and shrieking with joy. You were so much fun to watch!

We sat down at the table to eat. But before Easter dinner, I like everyone to hold hands as we say grace. I thanked God for the joy of family, the privilege of having friends, and, of course, I always say a prayer of thanks for having you in my life, Ellie. Once grace was finished, everyone began to eat. You were obviously very taken by all this. You yelled, "Stop!" Then you held out your hands on each side. It took us a minute to realize you want everyone to hold hands again. "All the guys, you too, Gwandma!" you said. So we all held hands again and then let go. We did this many more times. What fun! Ellie rules! You turned a great day into a treasure—one we'll never forget.

And we all smiled!

Love ya, honey.

Grandma Bea Goode

CHAPTER 22

Get Your Ducks Lined Up

April 30, 2007

Hi Little Elliott Jane, My Little Ellie Cat,

I babysat you today. We had great fun. For Easter you were given a set of little ducks for the bathtub. You didn't want to wait until tub time to play with them, so we took them out in the living room.

The little ducks are so cute. Each of them has a personality. One has a pirate hat and an eye patch, one has a tuxedo, one has a baseball cap, and one has a rain suit and hat, etc. We played and played. We named all the ducks. We called the tuxedo guy "Tux," the guy with the sailor outfit "Sonya," the guy with the rain suit "Rainy Day," and so on. We enjoyed our usual afternoon tea party. We made up songs about the ducks. Sometimes we fell back on old favourites like "Six Little Ducks That I Once Knew." We put the ducks in a straight line, in a three-line placement, in a circle, etc. We had a ball.

After I got home from your house, Mommy called me on the phone. You were having a meltdown. You and Mommy were playing with the ducks, but Mommy couldn't find the duck named Sonya! Mommy didn't know we were going to name the darn ducks! I told her that Sonya wore the sailor outfit, and soon all was well with the world again. Mommy and I shared a relieved giggle.

An hour later, I received another call from Mommy. She said that you told her we had brought the neighbour's cat into the house and petted her. Ellie, we did not! We did pet that cat, but weren't we outside when we did this?

Love ya, little fibber.

Grandma Bea Goode

CHAPTER 23

That's Just What We Will Do

May 11, 2007

Hi Ellie,

You had your second birthday party a few days ago. You loved it! You got to go to the Jungle Gym with all your little friends. What a place to run! It was so much fun. The next day you woke up and said to Daddy, "Go to gymnastics?" You became quite insistent, and why not? Poor Daddy had to work really hard to make you feel better, but eventually you understood. It was Sunday and the Jungle Gym was closed. It would be dark at the

Jungle Gym with no one around. So... okay, okay, you would go to gymnastics another time.

You are talking so much. Yesterday, I took you for a walk in the rain. We dressed for the occasion with rain jackets, rubber boots, etc. As we were walking along the side of the road, we found a mud puddle. You love to throw rocks in puddles, so we spent some time doing just that. Then we moved on. After a fairly long hike, we came across another mud puddle. It was ten feet ahead of us. You picked up a rock. I said, "Let's go throw that rock in the mud puddle." But you had other ideas. "No, Gwandma, go back, go back. Throw in *that* mud puddle," you said. "Sure, we can," I said. "If Ellie wants to go back, we'll go back. If that's what Ellie wants to do, that's just what we will do."

After I arrived home, Mommy called me to tell me that you had asked to go for a walk. Then you proceeded to answer your own question with, "Sure you can, Ellie. If you want to go for a walk, that's just what we will do." Mommy said that she could hear my voice when you answered like that... Heh, heh, heh!

Love ya, honey.

Grandma Bea Goode

CHAPTER 24

Greased Lightning

May 18, 2007

Hi Little Ellie, My Pally,

Last week I took you to the playground. You are such a little daredevil. You played on the little kids' slide. That was fun. You went up the ramp, made a turn, walked over the bridge, and then slid down the slide. I caught you as you slid down. When you reached the bottom, you saw the big kids' slide out of the corner of your eye, and you were across that playground and up that ladder so fast I couldn't keep up with you. You stood up on the top platform and were preparing to come down the big slide when I started yelling at you, "Wait, honey. Don't go down. Wait for Grandma!"

I saw you at the top of the slide and made a beeline for the bottom. I almost made it, but you were coming down like greased lightning. I lunged for you and missed. You shot out the bottom of the slide and kept going at least another four feet. You landed on your bottom. I ran to you expecting to find you crying. "Did that scare you, honey?"

"No. Was fun, Gwandma! Was fun!" you replied.

We left soon after because, with my heart beating so fast, I started to feel like I had just aged another ten years.

Mommy called me to say she took you to the park the next day, and again you made a beeline for the big kids' slide. Mommy said, "Wait until I get to the bottom of the slide so I can catch you." Apparently you waited this time... until you both said, "Go." Then you shot down the slide like a rocket. Mommy said you loved it.

I can hardly wait to try that sliding trick again... the right way.

Love ya, my little daredevil.

Grandma Bea Goode

CHAPTER 25

The Leaping Soap

May 23, 2007

Hi Little Ellie,

I babysat you today. We had such fun! I went to you in the morning. First, we played with your little people: Elmo, Zowie, Bert, and Ernie.

Then we made banana muffins. We had flour from one end of the house to the other.

After that, we decided to watch Diego on your car TV. But it wouldn't work so we decided to go to my house to watch it.

At my house you enjoyed a few minutes swinging on my bead curtains. You pretended you were Dora, and then Diego, and you swung back and forth and around in circles. What fun!

Before lunch, we played with my puppet dog, which you love.

After lunch, it was time to wash our hands. At your house, you use a bottle of liquid soap for hand washing, but I have a bar of soap in my washroom, which interests you. First you wet your hands. Then you reached for the bar of soap. You held it in your hands all right, but soon it took on a life of its own. That soap literally leapt out of your hands and across the room. It surprised me and I let out a yelp. I picked up the soap and placed it back in the basin. You thought this was *so* funny. What a belly laugh you have! We fought with that soap for a full five minutes. The soap kept getting away from us and you kept on laughing. We hated to stop, but our hands were beginning to look like raisins.

Your adventure today was to stand in my bathtub, pull the curtain closed, and peek around one end of the shower curtain. Then you would run to the other end and peek out from there.

Soon we were ready to settle down and watch our movie, but before we could start, we had to play "go in and out of any and every closet you can find."

At last, we put the comforter on the floor, found two big fluffy pillows, a soft, light blanket to cover us up, and we settled in to watch Diego. You started to play with my hair. I woke up several times… snoring. We were so relaxed and chilled out. It was wonderful.

When we got back to your house, we put on rock and roll music and danced like superstars. Then you pretended to be a cat. I think you must have been watching a cat show. You picked up Ernie from the couch with your teeth and carried him over to the window ledge to drop him off. Then you picked up Bert. You dropped him on the window ledge but decided to pick him up again and return him back to couch. This game went on for quite some time. You are so fun!

I sat you in your high chair for a snack of peanut butter in tiny wafer cups. I drizzled the wafer cups with honey. You informed me that Ellie likes honey! So we had lots of it. Soon Mommy and Daddy came home and it was time for me to go.

My heart was full, and I smiled all the way home thinking about our day.

Love ya, honey bee.

Grandma Bea Goode

CHAPTER 26

Let Me In, Let Me In

May 28, 2007

Hi Little Ellie,

On Monday, I brought you to my house. We had so much fun! As per usual, you played "run through the bead curtains" for a while and then spent some time going in and out of my little closets. Finally you headed to the cold cellar closet. "Flashlight, Gwandma!" I handed you a flashlight. We love standing in the closet and following the light. This time you grabbed my hand. "You get out now, Gwandma!"

"Okay, I'll get out." Then I knocked on the door. "May I come in?" I asked. You replied, "Ellie stay in, Gwandma stay out!" So I did. Then I knocked on the door. "Let me in, let me in." You thought this was so funny. You decided to organize us a little differently. You came out of the closet, stood outside, and shoved me in. You closed the door. Then you knocked on the door. "Let me in, let me in!" you yelled. I did. And we laughed. You are so much fun. You really do light up my life.

It was raining today, but we had a ball. I had bought you a little lawn chair. It is metal and has its own cushion. We brought it into the house, set it up in the rec room, and watched Diego. Then we had a picnic on the coffee table, using the lawn chair.

Eventually, you got tired and wanted to go home. And if that's what Ellie wants, that's just what we will do. When we arrived at your house, you could hardly wait for your nap. You went down like a lamb. What a treat.

Love ya, honey.

Grandma Bea Goode

CHAPTER 27

Eye Contact

May 30, 2007

Hi Little Ellie,

Auntie Sarah just phoned and we talked about you. You are now two years old and starting to assert your independence. At times, you've become a little unruly. You want what you want—now.

Sometimes you want to climb up on top of the piano. Mommy says, "No!" And your response is "Yes!" Mommy says, "No, no!" But you climb up onto the top of the piano in spite of all the requests. It is a big piano, and it frightens us all when you crawl up there.

Last night, while on the phone with Auntie Sarah, Mommy explained that you had been given a time-out. Auntie Sarah asked how a time-out is accomplished. Mommy told her how she's been attempting this discipline by sitting you in the big chair and holding her arm across you so that you can't get down... which you hate.

Then Mommy explained that it is very important that the parent refrain from making eye contact with the child for the duration of the time-out.

Auntie Sarah told me that while Mommy was explaining the time-out process and the necessity for the lack of eye contact, she could hear a little voice in the background saying, "Eye contact, eyyyyeeee contact." Auntie Sarah thought this was one of the funniest things she has ever heard. We are on Mommy's side in whatever preventative measures are necessary to keep you from climbing on top of that piano, but oh, Ellie, how you make us laugh.

Eye contact you later.

Grandma Bea Goode

CHAPTER 28

The Chocolate Pudding Fiasco

July 10, 2007

Hi Little Elliott Jane, My Little Ellie Cat,

I babysat you today. You were tired in the morning so we cuddled and watched television. Then we thought it might be fun to make some chocolate pudding with whipped cream on top. It was fun! You didn't like the taste of the whipped cream, but you sure loved the chocolate. You had chocolate all over you, in your eyes, in your nose, and in your hair. You looked like a little chocolate Easter cat... and somebody had to clean that cat up.

We decided it was time for a bath in the kitchen sink. The kitchen sink is small, so this was a new experience for me and for you. You discovered that the faucet could be used as a mirror and you got a great kick out of looking at your chocolate-covered face.

You hopped out of the sink looking refreshed and shiny clean. I, on the other hand, looked anything but refreshed. My shirt was wet with chocolate stains, my hair was in disarray, and my hands looked like shrivelled-up prunes.

You went down for a little nap after your sink bath. When you awoke, we packed up a picnic lunch and headed for the park. We unpacked our blanket and snacks and made ourselves comfortable under a big oak tree. "Who lives in the hole in this tree?" you asked me. "I don't really know, Ellie. Maybe a squirrel or a bird."

"Oh, Gwandma," you said, "a chipmunk lives in the hole!"

"Is that so, Elliott Jane? If you knew a chipmunk lived in that hole, why did you ask me? Was it just to trick me?"

"Yess!" You laughed.

After our picnic, we decided to check out the water. You are an actress all right, a drama queen par excellence. After you jumped into the water, you started playing an imaginary game. You immediately jumped out of the water and ran up and over the sandy beach until you reached the tree line about twenty feet away. You stopped beside our tree, turned and looked at me, put a hand on each cheek, and yelled, "Gwandma, Ellie must run back into the water!" You ran as fast as your little legs could carry you to the water's edge and gingerly jumped into the water. You turned again and looked at me. "Gwandma, Ellie must run back to the tree!" And off you went. You seemed to love this game, and we played "watch Ellie run" over and over again. It turned into "Here comes Ellie. She is going into the water! Now Ellie is coming out of the water! Now Ellie is running up the hill." We both found this hilarious and we passed the next hour laughing.

It was getting late and nearly time to go home. But you had made a new friend. He was a caterpillar named Hank, and you did not want to leave him all alone on the beach. Finally, I was able to convince you that Hank was going to be okay and that it was safe for us to leave.

When we got back from our outing, Mommy was home, and we all ate supper together. We had chocolate pudding and whipped cream for dessert. You drew a face with the pudding on the high chair table. Mommy laughed and added two eyes and a nose. Then you painted your belly, your legs, and your toes. Mommy took videos of you covered with chocolate pudding. "Ellie take shower, Mamma. Ellie take shower," you exclaimed. "Good idea!" Mommy and I agreed.

As I drove home, the memory of you in the sink, on the beach, and covered with chocolate stays with me, and I smile all the way home. How I love my little granddaughter.

How I love my Ellie.

Grandma Bea Goode

CHAPTER 29

The Whale

June 15, 2007

Hi Little Elliott Jane,

I was looking after you this week, and we talked about our plans to visit Science North on the weekend. You were very excited for this weekend. "Satiday, Satiday," you said. You grabbed my hand and shouted with glee, "See whales, Gwandma. See whales on Satiday."

"Are you saying whales, Ellie?" I asked. "I don't think they have whales at Science North, honey." You ran to your toy shelves and pulled out all of your stuffed toys: a lamb, a bear, a pig, a duck ... and a whale. "Whale, Gwandma! Whale!"

"Okay, honey," I laughed, "maybe we will see a whale."

At Science North, you loved the running space. Mommy yelled, "Ellie, put your hands in front of you, not behind you!" And you ran. You went up and down the stairs, hid in dark corners, and peeked through fences. You loved the penguin show and the penguin slide. You loved the snakes and the turtles. But most of all, you loved the butterflies. What would a visit to Science North be without stopping to see the butterflies? You were very gentle and soft with them. You were able to reach out and lift the butterflies onto your finger. On one of your reaches, you stopped in midstretch and gasped. "I've got hands!" you exclaimed, looking at Mommy. "Yes, you do," said Mommy. "I have hands too." You ran over to me holding out your hands the whole way. "Look, Gwandma, look. I've got hands. I've got hands!" You were absolutely amazed by this. You kept on looking at your hands. Then you gasped again. "I have hands, Gwandma."

"Yes," I said, "and I have hands too, and I can use them to give you a high five!" And I did. And there we were—you, Mommy, and I—smiling as big as Moses while we made the biggest discovery of our lives in the butterfly section of Science North.

And did we see any whales? When we got to Science North on Saturday, the first thing we saw was a picture of a whale and then a whole display of whales (orca whales) and a skeleton of a whale that went from the basement to the sixth floor. We were admiring the jaw, which was the size of a living room. You grabbed my hand and said, "Whale, Gwandma."

That's for sure, baby Ellie, my pally, smart-as-a-whale baby Ellie.

Love ya, honey.

Grandma Bea Goode

CHAPTER 30

Today Is My Birthday

June 18, 2007

Hi Little Ellie,

Oh, Ellie, you are such fun and so beautiful. Even at two years old, you are kind and loving and fair. If you hug me, you always make sure you hug Mommy too. If you hug Mommy, you make sure you hug me too.

The other day, Mommy asked you to come to the kitchen. "Kitchen, kitchen!" you said. "Go through the flowers, over the bridge, past the stove, and you will come to the big mountain where Mommy is!" You proceeded to act out this whole scenario, talking the whole time. You rolled down onto your belly and pretended to smell the flowers. "Over the bridge. Climb. Climb. Past the stove, and I come to the big mountain—where Mommy is!" You and Mommy laughed!

Last week when you and I were visiting the playground, you climbed up one of the ramps and were about to go over the bridge when you stopped and yelled to me, "You be the troll, Gwandma, okay?"

"Okay, Ellie, Grandma will be the troll."

"Say 'on your mark, get ready, get set, go!' Okay, Gwandma?" you directed. I repeated, "On your mark, get ready, get set, go!" And you ran across the little bridge. We both found this fun, so we repeated this scenario many, many times.

We left the park and went home to watch television for a while. The lady on the TV held up her magic mirror and said, "I see Bobby and Mary and Elaine. And I would like to say happy birthday to Tommy and Lisa and Ellie." You gasped! "It's my birthday! It's my birthday!" And we did a little dance. We lit a sparkler, and I wrapped up a little present for you to open. "I love birthdays!" you said.

And I love you, little Ellie, my pally, little "today is my birthday" girl.

Grandma Bea Goode

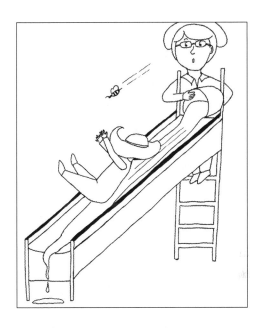

CHAPTER 31

Come on Down

June 20, 2007

Hi Little Ellie,

We went to the park again today. What a wonderfully warm month we're having! We had great fun on the beach, putting our feet in the water. You loved sneaking up on the seagulls.

I watched you and smiled until I saw you take off like a little bullet. You, once again, spotted the big kids' slide. It was 31°C today—hot, hot, hot! On a day like today the slide gets really hot.

"No, Ellie, don't climb up on the slide." But you had already made it up the ladder and were standing on the top platform. You like the big kids' slide, not just because it is bigger and faster but because it has a doughnut opening and you can get a grip on the sides. "Okay, Ellie, come on down."

"No, Gwandma. It is too hot!"

"Well, yes, it is, Ellie, but I can't climb up there and you have to come down, honey."

"But, Gwandma, it's hot!"

"Okay, honey," I said, "go over to the other slide on the middle platform. You can slide down that one." The other slide was not as fast or as hot as the big one, and it didn't have the doughnut opening at the top for you to go through. You were no longer filled with confidence. "Come on down, Ellie."

"No, Gwandma," you said hesitatingly. Oh, oh. "Okay, Ellie, Grandma's going to come up."

"No!" you said. "Gwandma not come up!"

Well, there we are between a rock and a hard place. Once more, I pleaded, "Ooookaaay, Ellie, slide down, honey."

"No, Gwandma, it is too hot!" You went back to the big slide again.

"Look, Ellie," I said, "I'm going to go get some water. If I pour water on the slide and you come down fast, it won't be so hot, okay?"

"Okay," you said. And off I went to get some water. All I had was my drinking bottle, but I filled it up and poured it on the slide. "You have to come down fast, Ellie!" And boy, did you ever come down fast—like greased lightning! I ran to the bottom of the slide and attempted to catch you. You came flying off the slide and into my arms, knocking me off my feet and causing me to fall backwards onto my bum.

We were both quiet for a minute. I had the wind knocked out of me. When I could finally speak, I asked if you were okay. Oh yes, you were okay. That was fun. Then we looked at each other and we laughed and laughed.

Brave, brave little girl. I'm so very proud of you. You are so smart and you are so brave. I am honoured to be in your company.

Love ya, honey.

Grandma Bea Goode

CHAPTER 32

It's Daytime, Gwandma

June 25, 2007

Hi Little Ellie,

Today we spent our last day of the season together. I loved it. Mommy fed you breakfast. You were clinging to her like a little monkey. You would curl up into a little ball and grab her hair and smell it and then cuddle tight into her arms. Oh my! She had a hard time going to work this morning. After she left, you were still pretty clingy. So you and I cuddled. You were happy as a clam, warm, dry, and with a good breakfast in your tummy. "I ate it all!" you told me.

We watched Diego. Then I thought that it would be a good idea to go outside and catch some rays. You would not let me catch you to put your diaper on. It was like trying to catch a rabbit. You would twist and turn and run and laugh. Finally, I pinned you down. You were mad, and I was frustrated. "Oh," I said, "you are such a gooseberry!" You looked me in the eye and burst out laughing! "Again, Gwandma, again."

"Gooseberry!" And off you would go again into peals of laughter. Finally we got you into your diaper.

"Go to playground, Gwandma?" If that is what you want, honey, then that's what we will do.

We played on your favourite slide (which nearly gives me a heart attack). You're so funny as you climb the ladder saying, "Foot, hand, foot, and hand!"

Afterwards, we went home to have lunch. You were hungry. You lay down with Daddy, who was on night shift this week, and he read to you. You could not settle for a nap. Daddy said, "I think Ellie is tired but she just can't go to sleep." I knew that I was tired. So you and I lay down. I waited while you searched through my hair with your hand until you found the perfect piece for twirling around your finger. Around and around your finger it went, and when I started to feel the flick, flick, flick that you do once you've sufficiently wound my hair, I knew we were on our way to sleep.

We both slept for a short while, and I awoke when I heard you say, "It's daytime, Gwandma! It's daytime!" Well, so it was. We smiled and then we were up. I looked in the mirror. My hair looked like it either got caught in a windstorm, or I stuck my finger in a light socket. I tried to comb it, but to no avail. Hair, hair! Ellie sure likes hair... and I sure like Ellie.

Love ya, honey.

Grandma Bea Goode

CHAPTER 33

Monster Baby

July 6, 2007

Hi Little Elliot Jane, My Little Ellie Cat,

I babysat you today. When your mom called to ask me if I would come out to babysit, I hesitated for about three seconds. I was feeling my age today, a little tired and achy from arthritis. *But no*, I thought, *Ellie is such a good baby and I love to babysit. It should be a piece of cake.*

A piece of cake, all right! Today my sweet, obedient Ellie had been replaced with monster baby, and I soon realized what I was in for.

I arrived at your house excited to see you; as usual, you were excited to see me. I love your big toothless grin. I believe your mom is getting nervous that those teeth are never going to come in, but you and I know they will. We also know that those gums are *strong*... especially if you sink them into skin. But we'll save that story for another day.

It was hot today, 28°C, and humid. I was quietly lounging on the couch watching you play. *Oh*, I thought, *isn't that cute? Ellie is trying to move her toy box away from the piano.* The toy box is situated beside the piano, and both are backed onto the wall. I remember thinking, *Man, she's strong to have moved that toy box*, and went back to reading my book.

When I looked up again, you were trying with all your might to move the piano away from the wall. "Don't do it, Ellie!" I yelled. There are plants, books, CDs, pictures, etc., on top of the piano, and there's an open electrical outlet behind it. You grinned at me as you successfully muscled the piano away from the wall. I was off the couch and running. I caught you just as you were about to poke your little finger into the electrical outlet!

Boy, you were upset that I would not let you electrocute yourself! I mean, what's the big deal anyway?! You had a total meltdown.

I decided to distract you by moving you away from the piano crime scene. We headed outside to play on the deck. There is a screened-in gazebo on the deck, which gave us some cover from the sun. The gazebo has a zipper that goes up and down. You reached down to the floor, found the zipper, and pulled it up as high as you could reach. Then you walked out of the gazebo pulling the zipper all the way down behind you. This allowed you to be on the deck while I was zippered inside the gazebo. My expectation was that you'd come back inside, as this is often the game. But *not* today, little honey. You didn't want to come back inside. So instead, you took off like a shot and headed for the edge of the deck, which doesn't have a railing yet. There is a five-foot drop from the deck to the ground, and you had no hesitation about wanting to jump. I reached you just before takeoff, and we both returned to the gazebo. You grinned at me, and I could almost hear those little wheels in your brain turning. "That was fun!" So you reached down and again yanked the zipper up with one hand, holding the other hand up to stop me from going through with you. Then you closed the zipper and took off running again, trying to reach the end of the deck before I could catch you. Oh my goodness, you little rebel! You make me laugh, but you scare me a little with your boldness.

I finally gave up. We headed back inside the house, and I began to make us some lunch. Daddy's stereo system is set up in the living room, and you went straight towards it. We put some music on, and you started to groove. You love music. You were tapping your feet, bopping your head, and trying to snap your fingers. I have never seen anything so cute!

I left you chilling as I returned to the kitchen to try to make some lunch. I had my back turned for about three seconds. That is all the time it took for you to discover the volume knob on Daddy's stereo. I thought I was having a heart attack as you turned the music up as high as it would go. The bass could have blasted us out of the room! You laughed with glee. Then you turned the music down as low as it would go. Ahhhh, peace! The next thing I knew you had turned the music up as high as it would go and removed the volume knob. You took off like a bullet, volume knob raised in your hand like a military salute. "Catch me, Gwandma, if you can!" Finally, finally, I did catch you and was able to remove the knob from your little fist of steel. I figured out how to reattach the knob, and at last I could turn down the music. It took me a minute to catch my breath and for my heartbeat to return to normal, monster baby!

We finally sat down for some lunch, and with our bellies full, we decided to have a nap. You don't have a favourite blanket like other babies do. Your favourite prenap comfort is to touch… my hair. But today, you didn't just play with my hair. You twisted it into tight little ringlets until it hurt, and then you would flick the ends of the ringlet with your thumb. This really relaxed you, but the same can't be said about me. "Please, baby," I prayed, "just go to sleep." I took a big breath. You took a big breath. And we were out.

The rest of the day passed uneventfully until Mommy came home. You wanted to show Mommy your new trick. I had never seen this trick before and was mortified. As we watched you, you shoved your fingers down your throat until you vomited. Then you laughed like you had done something really clever. Ugh.

"What! What! What's up with that, honey? Do you have sore teeth? Upset tummy?" Wait a minute... you have no teeth... and you told us your tummy is fine! I began wondering how Mommy is going to be able to curb your enthusiasm for your new trick.

Finally, it was time for me to go home. I got into my car, and I started to think about my day. I started to laugh... hard. I went home with a smile on my face and warmth in my heart that would carry me through until next time, when I would begin another adventure with my little monster baby.

Love ya, honey. You really do light up my life.

Grandma Bea Goode

CHAPTER 34

Peculiar Potty-Training Exercise

August 26, 2007

Hi Little Ellie,

Potty training has been a hot topic this month. You've been able to tell us when you have wet your diaper, but you still do not like to use your potty.

Last week you, Mommy, and I went shopping at Walmart. We were having a great time in the store when suddenly you asked, "Do you have to go pee, Gwandma?"

"Yes, I do, honey, now that you mention it."

Mommy grabbed your hand and off we went. You used the big girls' washroom and were as proud as punch!

When we arrived home, you continued your method of wetting your diaper and then telling Mommy about it.

The next day we decided to finish our shopping at Walmart. Once again you asked, "Do you need to pee, Gwandma?" Once again Mommy grabbed your hand, and we all rushed to the big girls' bathroom exiting with proud smiles. Hurrah for Ellie... who will only pee in the public washroom at Walmart!

Last night, you and I had our first "real" conversation on the phone. Usually Mommy instructs you to say, "Hi, Grandma."

"Hi, Gwandma," you say. Then Mommy will coach: "Say, 'I went to Science North today, Grandma.'" Then you say, "I went to Sci North today, Gwandma." But today, you'd been waiting to use your newly learned skill of whispering. You got on the phone, and in a whisper you said, "Hi, Gwandma. I have a secret."

"Oh, what's that, honey?"

"I have a new gate!" Then you hung up. Mommy called me back and explained that she had bought a new gate for your bedroom door so that they could keep Coco (your cat) from coming in, as well as keep you from going out. You've recently taken to exploring, and you've learned how to open the kitchen gate. Smart baby.

Auntie Sarah and I visited with you on Saturday. You hadn't seen Auntie Sarah in a while. Your name for Auntie Sarah has always been "Ari." But today your name for her is "Auntie Sarah." Auntie Sarah sat on the floor while you ran past her. Then she yelled, "Booga, booga!" And you laughed hard and screamed with delight.

We all went outside to play in the backyard. Without thinking, I said, "Let's run to the shed." And we began playing "On your mark, get set, go!" You'd repeat, "On your mark, set, go..." then you'd run halfway to the shed and purposely fall flat on your face on the lawn. Auntie Sarah joined in the game. You both waited at the starting gate with me, and once again, I said, "On your mark, get set, go!" Then you and Auntie Sarah took off towards the shed. But halfway there you stopped. "I guess that's as far as she wants to go today!" said Auntie Sarah. Then you looked up. Uh-oh! And off you went running again. Soon you had me running too. "Come on, Gwandma, come on!"

I was puffing. Auntie Sarah was laughing. "Why did you have to make the race all the way to the shed?" Auntie Sarah asked as we all fell down, laughing.

After racing, you stopped beside a wheelbarrow. Mommy had filled it with sand for you. "It's your birthday, Auntie Sarah," you said as you began inserting drinking straws into the sand. We all had to visit the wheelbarrow to take turns blowing out the straws as though they were candles. Then you brought us together and we practiced making our *p* sound—"puh, puh, pee"—and we all blew on the straws. We weren't sure how you connected *p*'s to candle blowing, but nobody made mention.

Auntie Sarah and I stayed late into the evening so that we could watch you while Mommy had a relaxing bath. "Watch me climb, Auntie Sarah," you said as you pretended to climb the tree Mommy has drawn on your wall. Then you convinced Auntie Sarah to lift you into your old crib. Jump, jump, jump, you love using your crib as a trampoline. Next you "nuggled" with Pooh Bear, Boots, and Teddy. Awww isn't that nice. Then you turned to Auntie Sarah and said, "Everybody is going out!"

"What?"

"Everybody is going out!" you repeated. So out of the crib flew Pooh Bear, Boots, and Teddy. We laughed. "I guess it's everybody out!" said Auntie Sarah. With all these toys gone, you had more space for jumping, and jump you did! Where do you get the energy? Did you not run to the shed and back enough times today?

Auntie Sarah and I went home, smiling the whole way. We love the fact that you gave us hugs and kisses good night.

We love ya, little honey.

Grandma Bea Good

CHAPTER 35

My Best Friend, Buzz

August 29, 2007

Hi Ellie,

I went to visit you today. You were upset because Mommy had killed your best friend, Buzz. You told me that Buzz loved you... sob, sob.

Mommy said, "We are not going to talk about it anymore. Mommy killed the horsefly. She feels terrible about it… She just didn't realize that Buzz and Ellie were so close."

Life can be hard sometimes, eh, little honey?

Grandma Bea Goode

CHAPTER 36

There Is Nothing Like a Narrow Path

September 12, 2007

Hi Ellie,

We hadn't seen each other in a while, and oh, I've missed you. You have become such a little character.

We spent a lot of time outside today. Mommy and Daddy have been putting in a new septic system, so the whole yard is bulldozed and the front yard has a mountain of gravel.

One of the things that you like best in life is a narrow path. So you and I decided to go to the side of the house in hopes of finding some paths to explore. "Come, come, Gwandma!" We made seven trips around the house, coming back to the paths each time.

Finally, we stopped in the front yard. The bulldozer had made at least eight narrow paths in the gravel and you were thrilled! By that time, I was a little tired, so I sat down in a lawn chair to watch.

"I'm Diego, Gwandma!"

"Are you, honey?"

"Yes," you said. "I save baby animals."

"Well," I said, "that seems noble and honourable." You approached me with cupped hands.

"This is a penguin, Gwandma."

"Hmmmmm," I said.

"I saved him," you explained. "He's back with his mother now."

"Why, that's wonderful, Ellie."

And off you went for another adventure. Again, you returned with cupped hands. "Here, Gwandma. This is a jaguar."

"Oh, lovely."

"Pet him, Gwandma!" And I did. You saved many animals today.

Later, you decided to go down your slide. There is a puddle of water at the bottom of the slide. I found an old dishcloth and wiped the water away. In doing so, three earwigs crawled out of the dishcloth. Startled, I jumped back and dropped the cloth exclaiming, "Ughhh!"

"But, Gwandma," you said, "they're my friends. They're my gooood friends! Earwigs love Ellie!" So we can't kill the earwigs, can we? I tried to find beauty in the earwigs, but man, it's hard.

By the afternoon we were both tired. Last night Mommy was going to read you three stories. She said to you, "Three books, that's all!" And she held up three fingers. Apparently, you reached over, grabbed her thumb and baby finger, and said, "Four, five books." So Mommy read five.

Because I was tired today, I kept falling asleep as I read. You cuddled into me and crawled up so you could lay your cheek on the top of my head. You twirled my hair. Then I heard you say, "I love you too, Gwandma." You always surprise me when you say this because I was just going to say, "I love you, Ellie!" Oh, it makes me smile!

We both fell asleep, and I thank God and my guardian angels for all the love in this room and for the extraordinary gift of a cuddle.

Love ya, little honey.

Grandma Bea Goode

CHAPTER 37

A New Jacket for Grandma

September 21, 2007

Hi Ellie,

I babysat you today. Oh, it was fun! But it didn't start off very well. You were asleep when Mommy left. Mommy snuck in to kiss your cheek. She tried to wake you, but you were way too tired. When you finally did wake up, you were okay for about ten minutes. Then you said, "Where is Mommy? She's here! I think she's in the basement!" So we had to have a talk about how Mommy snuck in and kissed your cheek and tried to wake you up. Finally, you seemed to accept that explanation.

We watched a bit of Diego on television. You love to answer the questions. Diego asked, "Do you see the mountain?"

"Yes," you said.

"How many toes does a jaguar have?"

"Four," you answered.

Once we were wide awake we decided to go grocery shopping. You wanted to ride in the car cart, and you did. You are so cute. You love to shop. We bought bologna for babies at the meat counter. Then we found cookies for kids at the baking counter. We were finished shopping before you were finished with your cookie.

You wanted to go to my house afterward because there are lots of toys there. We ended up playing in my basement sitting room for quite a while. You love to play in the storage room at the foot of the stairs. I left the light turned on for you. The door handle is only two feet from the floor, so you can easily reach it. "Bye, Gwandma," you said as you closed the door.

"Bye, honey," I said. Then you opened the door.

"Hi, Gwandma!"

"Hi," I said. You carried on this way as I stood near my bed folding clothes. Suddenly you realized that I have jackets stored in your favourite closet. You yelled to me, "Gwandma, Gwandma! I am finding a new jacket for you!" And sure enough, your little arms were reaching up, looking through the jackets. "Look," you said, "a new jacket for you."

"Well, thank you, little honey."

At the foot of the stairs I have a new mat. You noticed it right away by saying, "Oh, you have a new mat!" What an observant little girl you are.

You found a bag of small plastic people and furniture and a Fisher-Price pop-up toy. If you turn, twist, or move a button on the Fisher-Price pop-up toy, a corresponding figure of the same colour pops up. You had this mastered in short order and were having a blast with it.

We played on my neighbour's trampoline for a little while (which brought you a lot of joy), and then off we went back to your house with a bag full of Grandma's toys in tow.

When we got to your house, I was anxious for you to eat. I cooked you scrambled eggs with fresh green and yellow peppers. "I hate it!" you said. You were very definite. Sooooo... I cooked plain scrambled eggs in the microwave, which you usually like. But you were on lockdown, lips clamped, eyes averted. You were *not* going to eat. "I like apples," you said. So I gave you some of those. But by this time, I was feeling a bit frustrated. "It's that time of day when we go outside," you said. "We're not going out, Ellie, if you won't eat anything," I responded. "Okay," you said. You then got down from your high chair, went to your dollhouse, and hugged your little mice (they are about one inch high.) You played at your dollhouse for over an hour making up stories about going to the farm to see the baby animals. You talked to the mice. You had a tea party. I started to believe that you really weren't hungry until I caught a glimpse of you looking at me... making sure I was looking at you. I believe you may have inherited a bit of stubbornness from your grandmother.

Once we finally ate, we had some cuddle time. You made me read *Martina the Cockroach* three times. "It's my favourite, Grandma." You became sleepy and put your arms around my neck, cuddling into me. We love each other, and at this particular moment in time, all is right with the world!

Love ya, little honey.

Grandma Bea Goode

CHAPTER 38

Banana Splits

October 12, 2007

Hi Ellie,

We really enjoyed each other's company today. According to Mommy, you woke up at 6:00 a.m., stating, "Bugs Bunny is in the living room laughing and has a lot of friends with him." Excitedly, you and Mommy got up to check out the party. Therefore, you were tired this morning and I got to cuddle with you until you regained your energy.

Once recharged, we played "jump." You jumped on the couch, on Mommy and Daddy's bed, and on your bed.

Finally, it was okay to rest. You love to picnic, so I had set up the small table and chairs in front of the TV so that you and I could enjoy a good, old-fashioned TV breakfast. We ate oatmeal. I put a blanket under our table to catch the debris from our picnic, but even so, we had oatmeal everywhere, especially all over you.

I removed your oatmeal-filled pyjamas and was about to replace them with daytime clothes, but you slipped from my grasp. You love being naked. You love the feel of blankets and pillows on your skin. "I'm going to 'nuggle with Myles, Gwandma!" Myles is one of your favourite dolls. He is about eight inches high with yellow sleepers. Then you said, "I'm going to 'nuggle with Coco." Coco is your cat, and she was, unfortunately, not interested in 'nuggling with you.

Today, just because we could, we had banana splits for lunch. We took a plate and put a teaspoon of sugar in one spot, chocolate syrup in another, and strawberries and banana slices in the middle. We dipped our fruit first in the sugar and then in the chocolate and then we savoured it. You started giggling and saying, "Banana spwitz," like it was the funniest thing in the world.

This week you are really into contrasts. You said to me, "I'm going to dip the liddo tiny small strawbewwy. Then I'm going to dip the gweat big strawbewwy."

Mommy and Daddy had hired some friends to put a new roof on the house today. One of them, Ben, came in for a break; and I made him a coffee and some sandwiches. You were wound up and talkative. "Come, Gwandma, you can get my wabbit out of my cwib!... Look, Ben, I have a big, *big* wabbit." Ben laughed. "Yes, you do." Then you ran to your bedroom and took out a little stuffed dog. "Look, Ben, I have a little, little puppy."

I tried to get you dressed to go for a walk. You were pumped up and running, so it took a while. The sun was out for the first time in a week. You and I went in search of mud puddles. We found one and began throwing rocks into it. You held my hand so tightly today. I was in heaven. We walked up past the mailboxes and we played in the leaves. You like to make paths through the leaves. "I make good paths, Gwandma! I make vewy good paths."

"You sure do, honey." We headed to the top of the street. At the corner they have a little walkway. You love this walkway, so we stayed and played for a while. "You can't catch me, Gwandma!" you yelled as I chased you. You laughed and did not want to stop.

There was a small yet steep hill to climb down, so you had to go down on your bottom. "I'm going to catch you, Gwandma," you said from the bottom of the hill. And around and around we went. What fun! We loved it. Pretty soon you started looking a bit grimy. We took each other by the hand and headed back home. We had to make one stop for some toothpick twigs made out of straw. We found some good ones and put them in our mouths, just like the cowboys do on TV. You smiled at me and we were truly happy.

I love you, honey. I had a great day!

Grandma Bea Goode

CHAPTER 39

What Are You Doing?

November 7, 2007

Hi Little Ellie,

We spent the day together today. You were so funny and interesting. I arrived this morning with treats in my bag: Corn Pops (cereal), chocolate milk, and blueberry/apple scones. "We have lots and lots of chocolate milk, Gwandma!" Chocolate milk was on sale this week. Mommy bought two liters, Daddy bought two liters, and I bought two liters. It was a slight lack of communication.

You were very strong when Mommy had to leave for work this morning. I think it may have been because you were anxious for our picnic. I set up the table for you, me, Joanne (the doll), and Jerome (the giraffe.) "Do you like the scones, Ellie?" You are a picky little eater, but today you loved everything. "I do, Gwandma, I do like it." You finished your scone and then left the table to hide between Daddy's two guitars. "What are you doing, Ellie?"

"I'm poopin', Gwandma!"

"Come out of there!" I said. "We are going to go on the potty." Later, I noticed you mimic me. "What are you doing? What are you doing? What are you doing?"

After our picnic we decided to check out the snow. We found a large pumpkin. You brushed him off, cleaned his teeth, and cleaned his eyes. We laughed. You wanted to play in the backyard. I told you I couldn't because it's snowing and I have only my shoes on. You are becoming very independent lately and you said, "I'm going, Gwandma!" But you tripped. "Can you help me down the stairs, Gwandma?"

"Of course I can." I am thankful that I can still help you when you need it.

"I'm Shaggy, Gwandma!" you said as we walked down the stairs.

"Who?" I asked.

"Shaggy," you answered, "and you're Scooby-Doo."

"Okay then, I guess I'm Scooby-Doo."

You found a mud puddle to play in. "Do you want to go across the street, Ellie? They have great mud puddles over there."

"No, Gwandma. I'm not going."

All right then.

We went back into the house to have some lunch. I handed you some Craisins, thinking that you would not like them. "I do like them, Gwandma. I do," you said.

And you ate them all.

After lunch we played in the basement. We both like to paint. I tried to prevent you from mixing up the paints so that we wouldn't end up with only brown again. You made many handprints. We had paint everywhere. I laughed, "Don't touch me."

"I won't touch you, Gwandma."

"And don't touch the wall."

"I won't touch the wall Gwandma." We were really giggling by then with you looking at your hands covered in paint and me watching the paint dripping onto the floor. We headed upstairs for a serious scrubbing of the hands and found ourselves quite tired.

We crawled into bed. I read about African animals and our favourite—*Scooby-Doo: The Good Idea.* We snuggled. You twisted my hair so tightly you got your finger caught. We laughed and laughed until finally we fell asleep. You hugged me and my heart was so full.

I love you so much, baby.

Today was my Christmas gift!

See you soon, my Shaggy Picasso.

Grandma Bea Goode

CHAPTER 40

Don't Be Mean

November 17, 2007

Hi Ellie,

Mommy is off work, so I don't get to babysit you as often lately, but you came to my house this afternoon. We had such fun! We had several picnics and then decided to bake cinnamon rolls. What a mess! You wanted to "hep" (help) me clean up. You love playing in the water. You washed up for so long your hands started to look like prunes. "That's enough now, Ellie. Grandma's going to pull the plug!"

"Not yet, Gwandma, not yet!"

"Okay," I said, "one more minute."

"No! Gwandma," you said while grabbing the washcloth from me and turning your head.

"Heh!" I said sternly. "You be nice, Ellie. Don't be mean."

We continued washing for a minute more until you found a delicate china bowl. I took the bowl from you. "No, Ellie, not that one, honey. We don't want to break that. It's Grandma's special dish."

"Gwandma!" you stated. "Don't be mean!"

Got me!

Later, we put some music on and danced up a storm. What a great day.

Love ya, little honey.

Grandma Bea Goode

CHAPTER 41

I'm a Dog

November 21, 2007

Hi Ellie,

I babysat you today. We had such fun. We had a picnic of our favourites—pretzels and strawberries. You placed your pretzel on the table and tried to pick it up with your teeth. "What are you doing, Ellie?"

"I'm a dog, Gwandma! My name is Rags."

"Okay, Rags, let's clean up." So we went to the kitchen. I set you up at your own little table with a bowl of very soapy water and your plastic dishes. We had to refill the bowl with bubbles many times. We shaped bubbles, blew on them, and laughed! I gave you another bowl. You love to transfer water from the big bowl to another bowl using a small plastic cup. You think this is so much fun. By the time we were finished, I had to mop the floor and change your clothes from top to bottom.

Afterwards, we tried to have a little rest in your bedroom. You were determined not to have a nap. "We don't have to sleep, honey," I said. "We'll just rest."

"Okay, Gwandma. I'm going to 'nuggle with my cougar." Then you thought about this and said, "You can 'nuggle with my teeny, tiny bear, Gwandma." And I did. I read six or seven stories. We 'nuggled for a few more minutes and then we were up.

You were still a dog this afternoon, so I made dog bones out of apples. You loved it. Then I made a doghouse out of two chairs and a blanket. You went into your doghouse and stayed there for a long time. "What are you doing, Ellie? Are you pooping?"

"Yes, Gwandma. I'm not finished!"

"Come on out, Ellie!"

"No, Gwandma, I need to take my time. I'm not finished! Go away!"

Ohhhh... You're right, honey. Some things do... just take time.

When Daddy and Mommy came home, we said our good-byes. You gave me the loveliest hug and the nicest kiss on the cheek. I smiled all the way home and I'm still smiling as I write this.

I love you so much, my little honey.

Grandma Bea Goode

CHAPTER 42

No Tricks

November 28, 2007

Hi Ellie,

This week Auntie Sarah and I got to spend some time with you while Mommy and Daddy were at the hospital delivering your new baby sister. We had such fun. We played lots of jumping games. You love to jump. You are a jumping machine. Auntie Sarah and I tried to put fresh sheets on Mommy and Daddy's bed for when they would arrive home. It was hard because you just wanted to jump. You stood in the middle of the bed. I was on one side; Auntie Sarah on the other. "Do like this, Auntie Sarah!" you said while yanking her hand halfway across the bed. Then you grabbed my hand and pulled it towards Auntie Sarah's. "Hold hands." Then you proceeded to organize our other hands until we finally understood what you were trying to do. You wanted us to create a circle in which to jump in. You are a good organizer!

Later, you and I lay down for a rest. I read six stories. You played with my hair as I watched your eyes roll over and finally close. Ahhh, I closed my eyes. I was drifting off to sleep when I felt something cold on my nose. What was it? It was a nose. I opened my eyes and looked directly into a pair of big grey-green eyes belonging to you. "Santa is coming, Gwandma! Santa is coming!" you said excitedly—and we were up.

Later, I went to the hospital to stay with Mommy and your new little sister, Roxy. You'd already been to see Roxy during the day. Mommy told me you played with Roxy's arms. You would raise one of her arms up and then put it down… up and then down, up and then down. Roxy kept her eyes closed so you tried to open her eyelids—first one and then the other. "Ellie," said Mommy, "Roxy is not a toy, honey."

You went home with Grammie D and Granddad, and I picked you up afterwards for a sleepover at your house with Auntie Sarah and me. As I walked into Grammie D and Granddad's house, you came running. You hugged my leg and I picked you up. You hugged my neck. I laughed and kissed your cheek. "Did you see your baby sister today?" I asked. "Yessssss," you said. "But she doesn't do any tricks."

At your house we had another picnic dinner, this time it was Swiss Chalet. You love the potatoes. "I love butter, Gwandma!" You sure do, honey... and so does your grandma.

Mommy had brought you a new book: *Puff the Magic Dragon.* It has a CD that goes with it. We read the book and listened to the CD. You loved it. We sang and danced and waited for Auntie Sarah to come.

Auntie Sarah gave you a bath. "I'm a 'nake (snake), Auntie Sarah. 'Nakes go in the water. I sssss-lither. I'm going to ssss-care you!" You love to scare people!

Soon it was time for bed. Last night we tried to sleep with you in the middle between Auntie Sarah and me, but you were so excited by the novelty that you just couldn't go to sleep. You kept burying Auntie Sarah with toys. No one slept so we were pretty tired by tonight. We decided to try a new approach. You and I slept in your room while Auntie Sarah slept in the living room. I read eight stories, but you still did not want to fall asleep. You insisted that we do not turn your sleepy music on. It was getting quite late and we were all quite tired. "I am now going to turn the music on," I said. You had a little tantrum that lasted all of thirty seconds. Then we settled down, read one more story, listened to the music, and... and fell asleep. At last!

I love this time with you. I love you so much.

I feel truly blessed.

Grandma Bea Goode

CHAPTER 43

Meet Gwandma Bear

November 29, 2007

Hi Ellie,

This week everybody is a bear. There is Mommy Bear, Daddy Bear, and Ellie Bear. You joke by saying things like, "Gwandma Bear, Ellie Bear wants a cookie!"

On Monday, you and I were watching *Dora the Explorer*. Dora was visiting with her grandmother. Dora said, "This is my grandmother, my *abuela*! Can you say 'abuela'?"

"Abuela!" you said. Then you gasped and made a little sound like "Ohhhhhh!" You tapped your chest. "Ellie," you said. Then you pointed at me before coming over to pat my chest. You looked at Dora on TV and said, "My gwandma, Gwandma Bear!"

You are such a diplomat, so polite and you make me smile—and smile!

Thanks for the introduction.

Grandma Bea Goode

CHAPTER 44

I Do Have a Tub

December 10, 2007

Hi Ellie,

Mommy, Daddy, and baby Roxy had to go to the doctor today, so you came to my house to play.

The first thing you saw when you arrived at my house was the Christmas tree. I have the bottom branches covered with little miniature wooden figurines, and of course, little fingers are welcome to play with these. You made a beeline for the sunroom and opened the closet door. "I wov it here, Gwandma. So many toys!" You brought out every toy possible and then forgot them all as you helped me decorate (or redecorate) my tree. You discovered a long string of gold pearls. They must go on the tree! You draped and redraped the necklace around the tree. You were very serious about this task. Then you played for a while with my wooden ornaments and some glass ones, which were quickly broken. We laughed and swept. Then we decorated some more, particularly the bottom branches. No ornaments actually made it to the top half of the tree. When Mommy arrived later to pick you up, she laughed at our unique decorating style. She thought it was funny, but you and I thought it was a masterpiece.

After our tree decorating, we went to the basement for a picnic. We drank hot chocolate and watched *The Jungle Book*. We got a comfy blanket, a big pillow, and a soother (at your request). We cuddled and smiled at each other.

When the movie was over, you turned to me and said, "Gwandma, two ants were here."

"Pardon?" I asked. "Who was here?"

"Two ants were here. They came in and made me vewwy, vewwy dirty! Do you have a tub?"

"Surprise, surprise," I said. "I do have a tub."

"Can I have a tubby, Gwandma?"

"Sure you can, honey." We filled the tub with bubbles. We carried all the plastic toys from upstairs. You love the step up to the tub almost as much as you love to bathe!

You insisted that I close the shower curtain. It feels so much like a tent in there. You love it. Finally, I had to insist that you come out of the tub. You looked like a little prune. "You little raisin," I laughed, "get out of there."

"I'm a raisin, Gwandma. I'm a shivering raisin." We laughed, and I wrapped you in a towel that I had warmed up in my dryer. You cuddled right into me.

You felt much better and we began getting ready to go home. I don't know what we are going to do about those ants though!

Grandma Bea Goode

CHAPTER 45

Pesky and Lesky Pay a Visit

December 29, 2007

Hi Ellie,

I visited you again today. We were glad to see each other. Your little friend Tess was there. You love her. "Gwandma, Tess is here! Tess is here!"

After Tess and her dad left, Mommy and I took you and baby Roxy for a sleigh ride through the snow. It was fun. You and I made snow angels, and we "cleaned" the car. We broke off pieces of icicle from the car and watched the sun as it bounced on and through the icicles, making patterns on the snow.

When we returned inside, you and I proceeded to do our favourite thing—picnic. We had hot chocolate with warmed marshmallows, cheese, crackers, and grapes. You loved it.

Soon we had to do the dishes, and lo and behold, didn't those two sneaky ants come again. "They made me vewy, vewy dirty, Gwandma!" You absolutely had to have a bath in the kitchen sink. Boy, those pesky ants come at strange times.

Afterwards, you were feeling tired. You wanted your soother. Before we lay down, I tried to get you warm. "Put these pants on, honey. They are nice and warm."

"Nice and warm, Gwandma? Nice, warm pants, Gwandma!"

Finally, we were in bed. We read your latest favourite book. It is an aboriginal story about Christmas. We looked at the pictures showing Jesus in a tent. "It is a teepee, Gwandma. Do you know what a teepee is, Gwandma? It is like a tent, only little." You hold up your thumb and forefinger. "Little, little…" You sigh. We put on the CD that goes with the book. We love the language and the sounds. You twirled my hair and I was in heaven.

What a gift you are, my child. God's greatest gift of all.

I love you so much it hurts.

Grandma Bea Goode

CHAPTER 46

Not Yet, Not Now, and Maybe Never

January 4, 2008

Hi Ellie,

Today the girls went on an outing. You, Mommy, Roxy, and I went to visit Mommy's friend Lynn. Lynn has three little girls; two were away, but the oldest one, Lorena, was waiting for you to come. Lynn and her husband live in the country, and Lorena was anxious for company. Lynn thought you might be shy because Lorena is older (4 ½). Introductions proceeded as we entered the house. You snuck up on Lorena, circled her hand, and said, "Hi! I'm Ellie!" I thought to myself, *Ellie has been practising this with Dora the Explorer for quite some time.* Lorena had a living room full of toys, including a large Christmas tree, which is surrounded by a little wooden fence. You loved the fence. You pushed it out, in, out, and in. Fascinating. You and Lorena played and played. We stayed there for three hours.

On the drive home you fell asleep. Once we arrived home I helped Mommy carry you, Roxy, and all your bags into the house. Mommy explained that you usually won't nap if you've slept in the car. "Do you think you could nap, Ellie?"

"Not yet!" you said. Mommy and I have come to know that when you say, "Not yet," it means "not now, not soon, and maybe never." It was nearly time for Daddy to come home from work, so I told Mommy that I would head home. She would be fine with her two girls for a few minutes. Suddenly, we heard a loud cry. "Nooooooo, noooooo! Don't go, Gwandma! Pleeeease, don't go!" I looked up and you were running down the stairs sobbing. "I want a nap. I want a nap!" My goodness. little honey, if it's a nap you want then that's just what we will do.

So you and I curled into bed together. I read *Puff, the Magic Dragon.* Your latest joy is to allow the story to be read once through, and then the reader (namely me) must make up a story from the last two characters. So we looked at the last page and saw Jackie Paper and his little friend—a little girl. "Tell a story, Gwandma. Tell a story!" Okay. "Well, Jackie's friend Suzie really needed a friend. She was lonely and Puff was lonely too. So Suzie approached Puff, the Magic Dragon. Suzie was very frightened but very brave. 'Would you be my friend?' Suzie asked Puff..." You started twirling my hair, which is always the sign that you're falling asleep. We closed our eyes. I'm not sure who fell asleep first.

You're such a little love, little no-nap girl.

Grandma Bea Goode

CHAPTER 47

Pesky and Lesky Come Again

January 12, 2008

Hi Ellie,

Today when I was visiting you, you turned to me and said, "Gwandma, those two ants came to visit me today."

"Two aunts?" I asked. "Do you mean like Auntie Sarah and Auntie Caroline?"

"Nooooo," you laughed. "Two *ants*," you replied, making walking signs with your fingers. "Hmmmmmm!" was all I said.

After lunch, I walked to the kitchen to do the dishes. "Can I come, Gwandma?"

"Of course you can, little honey." So you grabbed the mat in front of the kitchen sink and carted it away so fast it would make your head spin. Then you grabbed a kitchen chair and turned it around so the back was facing the kitchen sink. "Grandpa Bill says to do it like this, Gwandma."

"Okay," I said. You love to do dishes. I washed while you rinsed. You filled up a plastic cup and emptied the water into another cup. Then you picked up a bowl from the counter and filled it up with water from the second cup. Soon it was overfilled and we laughed. "The ants came, Gwandma. They spilled the water."

"Oh," I said, "those sneaky ants!" Then you spied a piece of leftover chocolate cake on one of the dinner plates, and quick as a flash, you shoved it into your mouth. There was chocolate all over your face. "Gwandma," you whispered, "it was the ants. They made me do it."

"Oh," I said, "those pesky ants!"

"Those ants, Gwandma, they came and made me vewy, vewy dirty."

"Did they?" I asked.

"Yessss…," you said. "They said I have to have a tubby in the kitchen sink."

"Did they say you had to have a lot of bubbles in the water?" I asked.

"Yesssss…," you replied.

So we finished off the dirty dishes and refilled the kitchen sink with lovely warm water and lots of bubbles. We placed a very dirty Ellie in the water, and you loved it. We turned on the cold water tap and you proceeded to drink a quart of water using a kitchen spoon. You put the spoon close to the faucet. The water splashed into the sink. It splashed onto your tummy. It splashed into my eyes. Very seriously, you told me that it was those ants again. "They are pesky, aren't they?" I said.

Soon it was time for your nap. I lay down with you and proceeded to read four stories. You whispered to me, "Those ants, Gwandma, they are my friends."

"Do they have names, honey?"

"Yessss...," you replied. "Their names are Pesky and Lesky."

"Hmmmmm," is all I said as you and I both closed our eyes. Soon everybody was asleep—you, Pesky, Lesky, and I.

Love ya, little ant whisperer.

Grandma Bea Goode

CHAPTER 48

The Cheap Plastic Shopping Cart

January 16, 2008

My Darling Ellie,

Last week, my friend Mary came from Manitoulin Island to spend a week with me. On Wednesday, we took you shopping with us. You love to shop and you took a real liking to Mary. We brought you to Zellers. As we were going through the store you spotted a toy shopping cart. As far as you were concerned, it belonged to you. It was quite cheaply made, and I kept thinking the wheels were going to fall off, but you loved it. It was made with a little compartment at the top to hold things, just like a big shopping cart. You immediately wanted to put something in the compartment, so, of course, we did. I bought us a package of beads to play with later... and I bought the cheap, plastic shopping cart too.

My friend Mary wanted to leave Zellers to go to the music store in the mall. She was looking for a specific CD. You watched her as she started to leave. "Where are you going, Mehwee? I'm going with you."

"No, honey," said Mary, "you stay with Grandma."

"No," you confirmed, "I'm going with you, Mehwee."

It took a bit of persuasion, but you were finally okay with Mary venturing off on her own for a few minutes... especially since you and I could play on the merry-go-round while she was gone.

When Mary returned, she started looking at shampoo. "What are you doing, Mehwee?"

"I'm looking at shampoo, Ellie."

"Why are you looking at shampoo, Mehwee?" You seemed to love to say her name.

"Maybe I'll wash my hair with it," Mary said. We all laughed. We were having a good day.

When we got to the checkout counter, we were tired and ready to go home. You didn't want to put your jacket on. I sat you up on the counter, and before you knew it, we were dressed and ready to go. You fell asleep quickly in your car seat. I always look at you in the mirror and think that you are the most beautiful thing that I have ever seen.

What a great day.

Love you, honey.

Grandma Bea Goode

CHAPTER 49

The Not-So-Scary Wolves

January 23, 2008

Hi Ellie,

Yesterday you came to visit at my house. Auntie Sarah was here. You were so excited. You flew to my little sunroom, pulled back the sliding door of my closet, and proceeded to haul out all of your toys. You wanted to show Auntie Sarah your hammer set. You hammered a plastic peg into a plastic board. The pegs are in the shape of a heart, a diamond, a triangle, and a circle. "I wov this toy, Auntie Sarah."

I bought you a new set of glass dishes with butterflies on them. Butterflies are my lucky sign, and I loved this little set of dishes. We had such fun filling up the teapot and pouring tea for the ladies.

After tea, you wanted to go downstairs to play. At the foot of my basement stairs there is a door that leads into a cold cellar. It is a little cold in there, but there is a warm carpet on the floor. There is an overhead light you can turn on if you want to. But you never want to turn it on. "Can I have a flashlight, Gwandma?"

"Of course you can," I said. Away you went into the cold cellar, flashlight in hand, closing the door behind you. Auntie Sarah and I waited. Out you came. "Come on in, Auntie Sarah."

"Okay," said Auntie Sarah.

"Come on in, Gwandma!"

"Okay," I said.

While crammed in the cold cellar, you showed us your light tricks on the ceiling and on the floor. It was really fun. "We're the three pigs, Gwandma."

"Okay," I said. "Little pigs, little pigs, let me in, let me in, or I swear by the hairs of my..." No time to finish.

"Run, Gwandma!" you yelled. "We have to find a new house!" So we all ran to the bathroom and huddled against the far wall. "The wolf came again, Gwandma!" you said while yanking on my pants.

Sometimes grandmothers are not as fast on the uptake as little tykes would like them to be. So...

"Let me in, let me in," said the big bad wolf. "Or I'll huff and I'll puff and I'll blow your house in!"

"Quick!" you yelled. "We have to find a new house." So you, Auntie Sarah, and I ran back to the cold cellar. We stood for quite some time in the dark with the flashlight on, when suddenly you turned and knocked on the door with your hand. "It's the wolf," you said. "He wants to come in! Come on in, Wolf!"

You pushed Auntie Sarah out of the way so that there would be enough room for you, Auntie Sarah, the wolf, and me. Then there was another knock on the door. Again you opened it. "It is the wolf's brudder," you said. "He wants to come in. Come on in, Wolf." So the wolf's brother came in to join us. You nudged me over a little so that we could make room for you, Auntie Sarah, the wolf, the wolf's brother, and me.

Then we heard another knock. You opened the door, went to the stairs, and picked something up with your hands. You returned to the cellar with hands folded, palms facing up, cradling your treasure. "Look," you said, "it is a teeny, tiny baby wolf." You handed the teeny, tiny baby wolf to Auntie Sarah and headed back out to the stairs, returning with another teeny, tiny baby wolf. You again passed your treasure over into Auntie Sarah's hands. Between you; Auntie Sarah; the wolf; the wolf's brother; the teeny, tiny wolves; and the pigs (who were apparently in the cellar the whole time—we just didn't know it), it is starting to get a bit crowded in the cold cellar. "See," you said, "wolves are not so scary after all!"

"You're right," I laughed. "But I'm a big, *bad* wolf!"

"But you're not scary at all!" you laughed.

"Are you a wolf, Ellie?" I asked.

"Yes," you said, "but don't be scared. I'm really not so scary after all!" And we all laughed as we left the cold cellar to start a different game.

My wish at the end of the day is to have one more day just like this one.

Love ya, little friend of the wolves.

Grandma Bea Goode

CHAPTER 50

The Loudest Amen

February 3, 2008

Hi Ellie,

Today, Mommy brought you and Roxy to church. We sat up front to be close to the playroom. You looked so cute. You wore your pink-and-white Manitoulin sweater.

All of a sudden, you love going to church.

You are the youngest participating church member. You love it when the congregation stops to shake hands and greet their fellow neighbours. You shake hands with glee, but you don't want to stop shaking hands, and you become quite annoyed when the hand shaking is over.

Today the student minister, Catherine, called all the children to come up to the front of the church. She asked them all to perform little exercises like putting your arms out wide like a tree, soaking up God's love; putting your hands in the air like you're soaking up sunshine; etc. You loved it and were right into it. Then she tried to organize a prayer circle, but being the little organizer that you are, you put together a team and started your own prayer circle. Soon everyone was following you. We were all laughing. Catherine was laughing too. Then with great dignity, she had everyone stop and say a simple prayer. The loudest "amen" was yours.

As we left the service you again got into the shaking-hands bit. I had to explain your newfound love of hand shaking to several people as you grabbed their hands and started to pump.

We went for a pancake breakfast downstairs after the service. You loved it. You bossed me around a little bit though. You wanted more syrup on your pancakes. "You missed a spot, Gwandma!" Heaven forbid, this will never do. I had to borrow more syrup from another table.

You wanted me to come home with you after church, so I walked with you and Mommy to the car. We held hands, you and I, and I am so full of love.

You are the sunshine of my life and the world is a brighter place because you're in it.

Love ya, honey.

Grandma Bea Goode

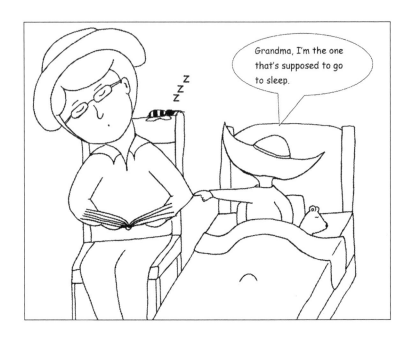

CHAPTER 51

Chockfull of Love

February 20, 2008

Hi Ellie,

We've been having girls' nights this week since Daddy is working evening shift. I've been spending the evenings with you, Mommy, and Roxy.

I arrived at your place around 4:00 p.m. today and began doing dishes and making supper. Of course, my little assistant was right there to help. You and I were making Swiss Chalet sauce. You were stirring but got distracted by the sink full of soapy water. So we had Swiss Chalet a la Dish Soap for supper. It was delicious!

You love to be scared. So part of the evening was spent exploring dark places with your trusty flashlight. "Come on, Gwandma. Come in here!"

"In here" is Mommy and Daddy's bedroom.

"It's dark!" you said. We checked out the clothes on the dresser. "Clothes," you said. We checked under the dresser with your light. "Mommy's stuff." Then we went to the bathroom. We had to shut the door and turn off the light. "It's dark in here, Gwandma!" You had me by the hand. You like to have company when you are exploring.

Soon it was time for bed. Mommy wanted to spend some quality time with you, so you and she played for a long time as I watched over Roxy. Poor Roxy was fussing and unable to settle. She had an upset tummy. So even though Mommy wanted to put you to bed, we decided it would be best if she took care of Roxy while I had the honour of reading you your bedtime stories.

I started to read about a little frog. His mommy asked him to get ready for bed. "No," said the baby frog. "I'm not tired yet." You looked at me with a twinkle in your eye. "That's just like me!"

I laughed because it is just like you. Lately, your favourite two words continue to be "not yet," meaning not now, not later, and maybe never.

After our story about the Gruffalo, you wanted to have a grown-up conversation. The story had ended with the clever little mouse eating a nut in the middle of the woods, and the nut was good and the mouse was safe. "One day," you told me, "not today, but the day before that and the day before that, I ate some nuts. That's when I was just a little, little girl."

"Did you, honey?" I said.

"Yes," you replied. "Daddy brought them. They were good."

"Did you crack the nuts open with your hands?" I asked. "Or did you use a nutcracker?"

"No," you said. "Daddy cracked open the nuts. He's very strong!"

"Is he?" I asked.

"Yes," you answered, "he has big muscles, and he eats a lot!"

You love your dad. It was finally time for lights-out. You twirled my hair, felt my face, and held on to my hands. We were quiet and peaceful. It was a blissful feeling.

Soon it was time to go home, and I left feeling chockfull of love... for you.

Good night, little honey.

Grandma Bea Goode

CHAPTER 52

That's Enough

March 3, 2008

Hi Little Ellie,

You came to visit me today. Your mom and dad are fixing up your house. They are putting in a new bathroom and a new bedroom for Roxy, so things are unsettled at your house.

When you got here, I had to go get groceries, so Mom and Roxy stayed at my house while you and I went to the store. You love to go grocery shopping. Today there were puddles in the grocery store parking lot. You could not miss that, so we were a few extra minutes getting home.

Because of what you're recently seeing with the house being renovated, you love playing carpenter. I have a plastic hammer and bench with designs on it. You spent a lot of time hammering "just like Daddy." You had to pause hammering for a moment to tell me a joke. "Why do hummingbird's hum, Gwandma?"

"Because their wings are going so fast?" I asked.

"No," you said, starting to laugh even before the punch line. "Because they forget the words to the song!" The joke was funny, and your laugh was contagious, so we both ended up laughing hysterically.

Later on, Mommy and I gave you and Roxy a bath. You love to bathe in my tub. You wanted your purse full of plastic toys, so I had to go and get it for you. You are getting older, and you are starting to assert your independence. As you were playing, you filled up a plastic toy with water and proceeded to drink from it. I was not comfortable with this, as I saw that the toy was now full of hot, soapy water. "Don't drink the water Ellie, okay?" You proceeded to gulp down some more. "Don't drink the water out of that toy, Ellie." You took another drink. "Ellie—," I began to say.

"Close the curtain, Gwandma," you interrupted as you closed the shower curtain and gulped down another drink. "Okay, Ellie, I'm going to take that toy. That's enough!" I said as I took the toy from you. You started talking to your other plastic animal friends in the tub and giving them heck. "That's enough! You heard what I said, that's enough!" Oh, I could hear myself in your words.

Mommy came in to find out what all the noise was about. Half of me was a little embarrassed and half of me was laughing.

Soon all was quiet again, and I bargained with you to get out of the tub. I traded your exit from my tub for a hot towel (which I create by throwing your towel in the dryer). You loved it. We cuddled up and laughed.

Gosh, you're fun.

Love ya, honey.

Grandma Bea Goode

CHAPTER 53

Not a Teenager

March 10, 2008

Hi Little Ellie Cat,

The carpenters are still working on your house. The really good thing about that is you and your sister get to come and visit with me. You've been getting a bit frustrated lately. Last week you were getting really tired of me and Mommy saying, "No!" and "Don't!" in phrases such as "Don't climb on that chair!" "No, you can't have a chocolate," "Don't climb on the tub!" You ended up stomping your foot at us and putting on your best scowl. Mommy commented that she thought she had years to wait until you started to act like a teenager.

Later, you were at my house having a bath in my downstairs tub. Mommy was with you, and I was looking after your sister. You started to yell out at me, "I am not a teenager, Gwandma!"

"You're not?" I asked.

"No, I am not a teenager! I am a big girl though. Before when I was a liddle, liddle girl, I used to play a lot with Mommy's hair. Now I just play with her hair sometimes!"

Oh, little honey, I love my teenager!

And I love my liddle, liddle girl.

Grandma Bea Goode

CHAPTER 54

The Mop

April 11, 2008

Hi Little Ellie,

It's been a long time since I've written.

Yesterday when I visited, you told me long stories. I love these stories. You told me that Grammie D. and Granddad babysat you a few days ago. Granddad took you for a long, long walk. You went to the forest. It was quiet. You could hear wolves there.

You couldn't see them, but you could hear them. One came out of the forest. He was a baby wolf, and he wanted to know which direction he should go. You told him to go towards the trees. What a lucky wolf he was to have found such an adequate tour guide.

Auntie Sarah was home on the weekend. You love when she visits. You and she had lots of energy. You wanted to tell her your joke. You do not say the letter *s*, so it was "Where do 'nowmen keep their money? Answer: In the 'now bank!"

You also love playing on your tricycle. There is a rope around the handle. Either Auntie Sarah or I would pull the rope while you gently pushed the pedals (or not), and we headed up and down and around the block. What fun!

Once inside the house, you and I played in your (s)paceship. You were convinced that I could fit inside. This spaceship is a big box with a door and windows—cut out by Mommy. I tried to fit inside and almost made it. I ended up feeding you your yogurt through the windows. I had to knock first and go from the front window to the back. You told me there were lots of holes in your spaceship and that I should look inside so that I could see them. You had made the holes with a pen. You made them so air could get in and out so you could breathe inside and outside. You know, you're smart.

After our bike ride and our spaceship adventure, you were tired. Sometimes you skip your nap, but today we rested. I read you three stores. My favourite (and yours too) is *The Emperor of Absurdia*. When the story was through, we made up our own stories about the creatures on the last page. "What happened to her, Gwandma?" you asked, pointing at one of the creatures. I began to tell you a story about a creature who had big eyes and beautiful, shiny hair. People loved to feel her hair because it was so soft. No one could be angry or upset around her... even the sad animals became happier around her.

"You have beautiful hair, Gwandma!" you said.

You had been playing with my hair for an hour. It was pulled, twisted, and twirled into little curlicues. I was very tired and nearly asleep. My eyes were tired and bleary. I sat up in bed, looked directly at you, and said, "My hair, Elliott Jane, looks like a *mop*!" You sat up and looked directly back at me. "It does, Gwandma! It looks just like a mop!" And then you started to laugh... hard... which made me laugh... hard. We couldn't stop. "A mop! A mop!" You chuckled. "It looks like a mop!" Mommy came into your room and asked, "Whatever is going on in here?" We tried to tell her, but we were both laughing so hard that we couldn't get it out. Finally, we explained my hairstyle to Mommy. She promptly agreed, and the three of us began laughing again.

Eventually we settled. I read another story. You continued to twirl my hair. You and your handmade mop closed our eyes, and we both went to sleep, to dream of the wonderful things they do in Absurdia.

Love ya, little honey.

Grandma Bea Goode

CHAPTER 55

It Starts With a J

April 29, 2008

Hi Little Ellie,

Daddy was on evening shift this week, so Mommy was alone during the evenings. Sometimes it can be hard for Mommy to divide herself between two beautiful girls who need her. So I've been coming to spend some time with the three of you. And I love it.

Tonight you were not feeling well. You have a cold. You felt hot all over. "I'm sick, Gwandma."

"Do you want a cuddle?" I asked.

"I do," you answered. And we did.

Before long, you were up and running. Mommy and I were doing the "Oh, oh, dance."

"Oh, Oh, Ellie, don't stand up on the back of the chair! It might tip over."

"Oh, Oh, Ellie, don't crawl up on top of the piano! You might fall off." You are active

and you make me smile.

Soon it was bath time. Mommy fed Roxy while I gave you your bath. You love to play with your Care Bears. They are plastic and about 1 ½" high. Tonight you gathered them together and saved them from a shark. You collected them in in a lifeboat (a plastic dish we have found for the tub). I think they were thankful.

I warmed a towel for you. It's not as good as at my house where I have a dryer in my basement right next to my bathtub. But it's pretty good if I run like a gazelle down to the basement, grab the warm towel out of the dryer, and run back upstairs to the bathroom. I think I should run a spa. I wrapped the towel around you and you snuggled into me. I love you so much. We put off getting dressed right away because I think we were both in the mood for a good snuggle.

The Secret Garden was on TV, and we got set to watch it. You love this show. It has a blue teddy bear named Igglepiggle and a gingerbread doll named Upsy Daisy. Upsy Daisy has interesting hair. Her head is surrounded by pigtails and when something interesting happens, the whole layer of pigtails jumps up and off her head, and the remaining pigtails stand straight up in the air. You love to watch it again and again.

"I think I know this program," I said. "I think I know their names. There's Igglepiggle and Upsy Daisy." You were still snuggled up in your nice, warm towel. "No, Gwandma," you said. "It's Higou Pigou. It starts with a *J*."

"Oh," is all I said. I stand corrected on the real names of the characters on *The Secret Garden* ...

I thank God and all my guardian angels for being able to spend this time with you. I think even grandmothers can learn how to pronounce Higou Pigou!

Love ya, little honey.

Grandma Bea Goode

CHAPTER 56

I'm Leaving Now

May 1, 2008

Hi Ellie,

Yesterday you came to my house for dinner. Mommy was helping me put a computer desk together. Shortly after you arrived, there were toys spread from one end of my house to the other.

We went down to the basement to play. I had left your flashlight on a low shelf and you found it right away. "I'm leaving now, Gwandma. I'm going into my house. Bye."

"Bye, Ellie!" I yelled. "Have a good time." You slipped down into my cold cellar, closing the door behind you. It was quite dark in there, but I could see your flashlight peeking through the crack in the door every now and again. Soon you came out.

"I'm back, Gwandma. I had a good time!"

"Well," I said. "I'm glad to see you."

"I'm going now, Gwandma. I'm going back to my home." Back into the cold cellar you went. We played this game many times. You're so much fun!

Love ya, little honey.

Grandma Bea Goode

CHAPTER 57

Gwandma, Be Bwave

May 2, 2008

Hi Little Ellie,

I got to spend the day with you today. You were hyper! It was cool out, and you had been indoors most of the day. Mommy seemed a little overwhelmed, so you and I went to the park. What fun! We had a picnic, fed the seagulls (which is a real no-no!), and then we snuck up on some geese. "'Neakin', 'neakin'," you said as we tracked the geese. You and Mommy had made blueberry muffins today, so we shared our picnic muffin with the geese.

You were very excited about the big slide. You crawled up the metal ladder to the first tier, which has the smaller slide (which I prefer you to use), and then you had to crawl up to the second tier, which is about ten feet off the ground. My heart always beats faster when I take you to the park.

The second tier slide has a doughnut opening. You love this because when you talk, there is an echo. So before coming down the slide, we always have a conversation. "I'm coming down now, Gwandma."

"Okay, honey."

"You catch me, okay?" I felt a little scared remembering the last time we tried to pull this stunt (which ended up with me on my buttocks). Down you flew like a bullet, while I only hoped to catch you. You exited from the bottom of the slide and continued flying for three feet. You landed in the sand on your feet, and I grabbed you, keeping you from falling backwards. You loved it! Oh, we laughed. We did this again and again.

After many times down the slide, you decided that I, too, should enjoy some of the fun. You insisted that I should take a turn on the slide. You tried to convince me to climb up the ladder, which isn't a ladder at all, only metal rungs going up.

"Come on up, Gwandma," you said from your perch on the first tier.

"No, honey. The slide is only for kids."

"Come on, Gwandma, you can do it!"

"No, Ellie, I'm not climbing that ladder."

You peered over the tier. "Come on, Gwandma! Just put your foot on the bottom rung. Then put your other foot on the next rung. Don't look down. You can do it."

"No, Ellie, Grandma is not going up there, honey."

Again with the "Just put your foot on the bottom rung, Gwandma, and push off. Then put your other foot on the next rung. Come on, Gwandma! Be bwave!"

But no, Grandma didn't want to be brave today, and in truth, I was a little disappointed that I didn't get to go down the slide. I worried that I might hurt my one good ankle upon landing. So I decided to stay grounded.

Mommy laughed when she heard the story. "Oh, great, Mom," she said. "That would be just great—the only two people in the park and you at the bottom of the big slide with two broken ankles. Sometimes I wonder about you girls!"

Hmm... sometimes I wonder about us girls too.

Love ya, little honey.

Grandma Bea Goode

CHAPTER 58

Don't Make Ms. Mistoffelees Jump So High

May 8, 2008

Hi Little Ellie,

I spent the evening with you, Roxy, and Mommy last night. I loved it. Mommy was making supper and washing dishes, so you and I went to change the beds. Our routine is to do one hour of housework, eat supper, and then play, bathe, watch TV, and go to bed. You and I were pulling the sheets off the bed. You love to jump on the bed. "I'm Ms. Mistoffelees, Gwandma."

"Oh," I said. "Hi, Mr. Mistoffelees."

"No, Gwandma, *miss*—Ms. Mistoffelees. You are Mr. Mistoffelees."

"Okay," I said, "jump as high as you can, Ms. Mistoffelees." And you jumped, again and again.

"Gwandma, you made Ms. Mistoffelees jump too high. She hurt her knee."

"Ohhh, sorry, little honey."

"Not 'little honey,' Gwandma! Ms. Mistoffelees!"

"Oh, that's right," I said. "Are you okay, Ms. Mistoffelees? Do you need a hug?"

"Yessss," says Ms. Mistoffelees. Thank goodness I got it right that time.

Later on, I sat you in your seat for supper. Out of nowhere you looked at me and said, "Brendan—he called me a boy." Then you broke down into sobs. I recalled the visit you had a few days ago with some of Mommy's friends and their children. Mommy had told me that you had been upset because one of the boys made a mistake in his wording. I tried to explain that Brendan didn't call you a boy. He just told his Mommy that, "Him was on his truck."

"He called me a boy, Gwandma!"

"No, little honey. He just gets the boy-girl thing mixed up. He knows you're a girl. Sometimes it's hard for kids to know who is a girl, who is a boy, who is a sister, who is a brother."

"What was your mother's name?" you asked between sobs. "Where is she? Who is your mother? Is Auntie Sarah your sister? Who is her mother?" You had a million questions. Finally, you seemed to accept that maybe Brendan didn't mean to call you a boy, and we had another cuddle.

Usually you are very independent and confident, but having a little sister is not always easy. Tonight, you seemed to want more than your usual amounts of hugs and cuddles. I thank God and my guardian angels that I am allowed to give them to you.

Love ya, Ms. Mistoffelees.

Grandma Bea Goode

CHAPTER 59

Paint the Deck, Gwandma

May 11, 2008

Happy Birthday, Darling Ellie,

You turned three years old today. Mommy and Daddy had a party with Grammie D, Granddad, Uncle Dan, Aunt Kate, and me. What fun! Daddy cooked chicken on the barbecue. When I came into the house, you were sitting in your booster seat, fork in hand, holding onto a paper teddy bear plate, waiting for your birthday cake. Granddad told me you had been waiting a long time. Mommy said you have to eat some supper first... uh-oh...

You were very pleased with your presents. I gave you a hobbyhorse and you loved it. It is just a broomstick with a horse's head on one end. "Get on, Auntie Kate!" Auntie Kate jumped on and away you went. "Get on, Gwandma!" And I did. Three on a horse is hard... and one of us fell off.

We went outside to find it was the most beautiful day. It was twenty-five degrees, hot, sunny, and there were no flies. Granddad had been cooking fish on his Coleman burner. He offered you a piece and you ate it. "I wuv it, Granddad!" I am amazed because sometimes you're a bit picky about what you eat. But you did seem to "wuv it" because you ate it all up.

Yesterday Mommy took you to a speech therapist to have you assessed because at times some of us have a hard time understanding what you are saying. You have an extensive vocabulary, and I think some of us are just old and hard of hearing. You talk well, but you have a hard time with the letter *l* and the letter *s*, and you have a very hard time putting an *s* at the beginning of a sentence. The speech therapist told Mommy that at least 75 percent of kids under three can't pronounce *l* or *s*. She also said that you have the vocabulary of a five-year-old and not to correct a thing. So, little sweetheart, we'll just continue on loving you and having the privilege of listening to our little New Yorker as she talks with an accent that is totally captivating and charming.

You, Auntie Kate, and Uncle Dan played a game of soccer. Then you discovered a shovel, and you wanted to dig up your garden, which is a two-by-two-foot area of soil. "This is not Daddy's garden, Gwandma," you said. "It is my garden!"

"Okay, little honey." The ground was hard. "Can I help?" I asked.

You responded with, "Don't wuwwy, sweetie, I can do it!"

"What did you say, honey?"

"Don't wuwwy, sweetie," you answered again, "I can do it. I can dig the garden." Okay then, I guess you can dig the garden.

I found some pretty rocks and made an arrangement with them. "Want to see, Ellie?"

"No, Gwandma. I'm busy," you said. Well so you are, little honey, so you are. You found two sponge brushes and a margarine container. "Fill me up, Auntie Kate."

"Pardon," said Auntie Kate.

Uncle Dan came to the rescue. "Fill it up, Kate, with water." So Auntie Kate filled up your margarine container. With the water and sponge, you painted my rocks and then the shovel. Then you passed me a sponge. "Paint the deck, Gwandma." So I did. You joined me and we painted together, and a mighty fine job we did too.

Soon we all went into the house to eat. You love to sing "Happy Birthday." "Happy birthday to me," you sang as you pointed to your chest. "Happy birthday to me!" Point, point. "Happy birthday, dear Elliott Jane. Happy birthday to me!" The room was filled with light and love. Grammie D and I avoided looking at each other because we knew our hearts were full, our eyes were teary, and our cups runneth over. We knew that if we looked at each other, we would be blubbering like happy fools, so we smiled through our tears and wished you a very happy birthday.

We love you, beautiful Ellie, beautiful little birthday girl.

Grandma Bea Goode

CHAPTER 60

Just the Three of Us

May 14, 2008

Hi Little Ellie,

So much has happened this week. On Sunday, Roxy was christened at church. She wore a long white gown with a white sweater. She was so cute and you—you looked beautiful. You had on a printed cotton dress that was a little long with a big pink bow around the waist. It had a crinoline underneath. You took our breath away.

All of our little family was at church: Mommy, Daddy, Aunt Kate, Uncle Dan, Grammie D, Granddad, Auntie Sarah, and me. Church is hard for little three-year-olds, especially for three-year-olds named Elliott Jane. You were curious, observant, and out of your seat. You went over to a big plant in the corner. I think you wanted to see if it was real... or perhaps you just wanted to know what it felt like. You touched the leaves, gave them a good rub, and then you smelled them. The next thing we saw was you trying to lift the plant, first by the base and then by the plant itself. I gave a little gasp, thinking my church was about to lose one of its nicer plants, but no, you decided to let it live. Whew. You returned to the pew and sat beside Mommy and Daddy for a minute. Then you came over to Grammie D and I. You pushed me down toward Mommy, and you pushed Grammie D closer to Granddad. Then you settled yourself between the two grandmothers. You hugged Grammie D and then you hugged me. But no, you were not entirely happy with this arrangement, so you pushed Grammie D next to me, and then you sat between Grammie D and Granddad. Granddad was beaming! You wrapped your little arms around his neck and cuddled in. We all smiled.

After the service, we went back to Mommy and Daddy's for a barbeque. It was a beautiful day, and we were all happy to be with you. As I came in the door, you greeted me with, "Hi, Gwandma, me and Mr. Mespi, Mephi—oh, what's his name, Mommy?"

"Mr. Mistoffelees," she answered.

"Me and Mr. Mistoffelees are going downstairs, Gwandma." You were holding him by one imaginary hand, and you obviously wanted me to take his other hand. So of course, I did, and down we went to the basement—just the three of us.

Soon we went back upstairs because there were presents to open and you love to open presents. There were paper bags all over. It was like Christmas.

It was such a beautiful day. We decided to sit out on the deck. In the backyard there was a plastic slide, and you decided to slide down face first. Your feet started to move up and over your back. I thought you were going to snap in half, and it scared me a little. "Ellie," I said, "maybe it's not a good idea to come down that slide face first." You were already crawling up on the steps of the slide. You got to the top step and very patiently explained, "Gwandma, it's just a liddle, liddle slide," and you demonstrated with thumb and forefinger. I laughed. "You're right, honey, it is just a little, little slide." You smiled and went down the slide face first just as you had planned.

Later, you took my hand and showed me the tulips that are growing in Daddy's garden. They are dark red and pretty, and they look so brave in the sunshine. They are an early reminder that summer really is coming, and they bring me hope. I smiled. My heart is full today.

On the way back to the house, you organized me again. You are a natural leader, and you are very good at getting people to follow your instructions. "You walk up the hill, Gwandma. I'll walk up the stairs," you said. "I'll meet you at the top." So that's what we did. Then we held hands again and took a little walk in the sunshine. And again, my heart smiled.

Our dinner was almost ready, so we went back into the house. Mommy asked me to hold Roxy for a while. As I was sitting and playing with her, you walked over to me. You suddenly looked very tired. You lay down beside Roxy and me. I asked Mommy if we could trade off girls for a little while because Roxy was hungry and needed her mommy, and you were tired and needed your grandma. I gently tickled your back. You loved it. I caressed your face and gently played with your hair. I lay down beside you. I was on the floor, and you were on the foam mat Mommy had laid down for Roxy. I covered you with a blanket and you snuggled in, eyes heavy, as you reached over to play with my hair. Peace gently descended upon us.

My heart is so full of love for you. I smile, again... I smile.

Love ya, little honey.

Grandma Bea Goode

CHAPTER 61

Little Treasure

May 20, 2008

Hi Little Elliott Jane,

I spent the evening with my girls again yesterday. It was a beautiful day: sunny, warm, glowing, like stardust on the wind. So after supper, you and I decided to go for a walk. We brought the stroller along just in case. You love to push it. Along the way, we picked up many treasures. You stored them in the mesh basket in the back of the stroller. We had a rock, two straws, a feather, and a stick. Not bad for a day's work.

During our walk, we went to the top of your street, where we stopped at our favourite little path. The path is even more fun than you might imagine because as you walk along, it inclines down dramatically and then flattens out. The path is narrow and fun to run along. As we reached the path, you informed me, "I am not Elliott Jane, Gwandma. I'm Velma." You've been watching Scooby-Doo, and Velma is a character in the TV series. "Oh, hi, Velma," I said. "How are you doing?"

You ran up to the path, ran back to me, shook my hand, and ran back to the path. "Bye, Gwandma!"

"Bye, Velma. Have a good time."

"I'll have a good time," you said and then ran to the end of the path and started back. "I'm back, Gwandma."

"Welcome back, Velma. It's good to see you. How are you doing?"

"I'm great!" said Velma and shook my hand again. "I'm leaving now, Gwandma."

"Bye, Velma, have a good time."

"I'll have a good time!" you told me, and then you ran to the end of the path and back. We played the "hello, Velma, good-bye, Grandma" game again and again.

Then you discovered a large amount of sand that had built up along the side of the road. You grabbed two handfuls of sand and distributed it as evenly as possible over the path. I was starting to get tired, so I suggested that we should think about leaving soon. "Oh no, Gwandma. I'm too busy. I'm so busy, Gwandma."

"I can see you're busy, Ellie, but we should think about going home before dark."

"I'm too busy, Gwandma. I'm vewy, vewy busy!" And you ran with your sand. I could see that you really were very busy, so I decided to wait until your job was finished before leaving.

Finally, your job was done. We headed down the road to the playground. "Okay, Ellie," I said, "we are not going down that big hill because if we go down, I don't know if I can get back up again before dark."

"I weally, weally wov to go to the park, Gwandma."

Ohhhh... so we went. We played on the slide. "Climb the stairs, Gwandma."

"Okay, I will but only once." (I remembered the last time I passed on my chance to take the slide). After I had climbed the ladder six or seven times, I had to be a little more assertive with you, so I put my foot down.

"We have to go home now, Ellie." But you were playing pirates and Captain Feathersword. We were halfway out of the park when you started to cry because you left your pretend sword on the slide and just couldn't leave without it. "We are leaving!" I said.

"Okay, Gwandma, but I am sad."

"Sad?" I asked.

"Yes," you said, "Captain Feathersword really needs his sword."

"Ohhhh... well, in that case, we better go back and get it." After retrieving the sword, you left quite happily. "I need to go in the stroller, Gwandma," you said. "I'm too tired to go up the big hill."

"Noooo," I said, "that wasn't the deal."

"Yessss, Gwandma," you said... and into the stroller you went.

Halfway up the hill I checked again. "Are you sure you don't want to walk up part of this hill, Ellie?"

"I'm sure, Gwandma," you said, and we continued towards home. You loved it when we reached the top of the hill (and so did I). I really wanted to get home before dark, so I made a game out of pushing the stroller as fast as I could. We made it down the other side of the hill in a flash. As we continued towards home, you wanted to get out of the stroller a couple of times to pick up more treasures, but eventually my little treasure and I made it back home—before dark.

Oh, little honey, you bring such light and joy to my life. As I write this I can't stop smiling.

I love you, Velma.

Grandma Bea Goode

CHAPTER 62

But... He's My Vewy, Vewy Good Friend

June 17, 2008

Hi Little Elliott Jane, My Little Ellie Cat,

Today I got to spend the day with you. We asked Mommy if I could take you shopping with me while she went grocery shopping with your sister. Off we went... but not quickly. We shut the door to your house, and you knelt down and picked up a caterpillar. "He's coming shopping with us, Gwandma."

"Oh no, honey, he likes it here at home."

"But, Gwandma, he's my vewy, vewy good friend."

"Your good friend, eh? Well, then, I guess he had better come with us."

So off we went... you, me, and your very, very good friend. "Does he have a name, Ellie?" I asked.

"Yessss."

"Is it Eddie?"

"No, Gwandma."

"Is it Frank, Ellie?"

"No, Gwandma."

"Is It Matthew?"

"No, Gwandma. It's... Wobert. It is! It is Wobert. My fwiend's name is Wobert."

When we got to the hardware store, you wanted to bring Robert inside. "No, Ellie, he needs to stay in the car, okay?"

"Okay, Gwandma." Thank goodness.

As we entered Home Hardware, you went straight for the fountain display. There were about ten little fountains. All of them are your height, and you had to stick your finger into each one. You just had to. There were fountains with lights, angels, rocks, and music. We were both fascinated with them.

Next we visited the toy department. You told me you would just "wov to have" every toy you saw, but I was determined to buy only one. We bought a pink plastic table to go with the pink plastic chair I bought you last week. Now you'll be well equipped to have a picnic on my sundeck.

Robert was still in the car when we finished shopping. Whew. I had to convince you that before we went inside my house, we'd first have to set Robert free. "All animals deserve to live free, Ellie. So just put him on a rock and let him go, okay?"

"No, Gwandma, Wobert needs to go in a puddle." So we brought Robert to a puddle, and we set the little fella free.

Inside my house you played, for a while, at your shelves in the sunroom, but you soon wanted to go downstairs and watch *The Jungle Book*. "But we could go outside to play, Ellie."

"No, Gwandma, I want to watch *The Jungle Book*." So we set ourselves up with a snack and settled in for the movie. You started off sitting in the big chair, but eventually we both ended up on the couch. We found a pillow and a soft blanket. You played with my hair as we watched Mowgli and Baloo. We were content. You wanted me to rub your back, and I did. We forgot the time, and before we knew it Mommy was there to pick you up and to take you home. You were not ready to leave yet, and it was quite disappointing for you. Next time I will try to prepare you a bit sooner, and I will watch the clock more carefully. You and I talked gently and decided that next week we are going to have a sleepover. I can hardly wait!

Mommy called me up around 7:00 p.m. You had been tired and cranky tonight. Mommy had to discipline you and tell you not to yell. "When I am at Gwandma's," you said, "she lets me do whatever I want to do."

"Uh-oh," Mommy told me. "She really has your number, Grandma."

Yes, you do, little honey, little love of my life. You do have my number.

Love ya, little honey,

Grandma Bea Goode

CHAPTER 63

The Unsleepover

August 14, 2008

Hi Little Ellie,

You get cuter and more interesting every day. This week you love to talk. I listen to you with excited anticipation at what you're going to say next. What an amazing girl you are!

We had an unsleepover at my house last week. You wanted to come, but you weren't feeling all that well. Roxy had the flu, so I suspected you may have been catching it as well.

Our unsleepover began with a shopping trip to Zellers. We bought a stool for you to stand on ("I want the green one, Gwandma!"), a toilet seat, a new toothbrush, tub toys, and Winnie-the-Pooh plastic dishes. I noticed that you weren't your usual energetic self because you actually sat in the cart at Zellers and let me drive you around.

I like to give you my undivided attention, so we stopped at a restaurant on the way home so that I wouldn't have to interrupt our conversation by cooking supper. In the restaurant, you kept wrapping your little arms around my neck and saying, "I wuv you, Gwandma! I just wuv you!" And *I* love you, little Elliott Jane!

After supper we realized it was necessary to make an additional stop at the doughnut shop since we felt that, being sick and all, we deserved it. I bought you your favourite treat: a vanilla doughnut covered with sparkles. It was fun. You are such good company... even when you're feeling under the weather.

When we arrived at my house, you had a bath with your new tub toys. We cuddled on the couch and watched *The Jungle Book*, and then... you got lonesome. "I want my mommy." Awww. Poor pet. So we packed up your belongings and went back to your house. I want you to feel very comfortable at my house and to know that you can come for a sleepover at any time. And I wanted you to know that if you felt homesick, you could always go home.

Last night you were feeling much better. I came over for supper with Mommy, Daddy, Grandpa Bill, and Mary. Gosh, you were fun. "Wanna see what I can do, Grandpa Bill?" you asked as you slid down the slide, ran around a ball, and "painted" the sundeck. As we were going to sit down at the table, you organized everybody. "Sit here, Mehwee!" Mary had the place of honour, right beside you. You wanted Grandpa Bill close, but he didn't need to sit right beside you.

Ever since Roxy was born you have been fascinated with pregnancy. "I have love in my tummy, Gwandma. I have a baby in there." Tonight, you told Grandpa Bill and Mary that Gwandma was going to have a baby. "Yessss, there's a baby growing in Gwandma's tummy, all right." Grandpa Bill and Mary seemed embarrassed. They thought you might be insulting me because I am a little (cough, cough) overweight—and I do have a nice, round belly. Everybody was trying to change the subject, but I thought it was pretty funny. For you, it seems to be all about love. If you could have love in your tummy, then I could too. Kids do say the darndest things.

I received a lot of hugs and kisses from you last night... in between watching all the things that you could do. One of the things you are proud of is being able to pick up your baby sister Roxy. Because you often try this trick, we have to keep an eye on you all the time.

Grammie D and Granddad have been away for nearly two weeks, and they are lonesome for you and Roxy. So that's where you're heading today. I could hear you on the phone while I talked to Mommy. "I love you, Mommy, and I love Granddad!" Mommy tried to direct your attention to all the other people in your life, like Grammie D, Grandma, Daddy, Grandpa Bill, Mary, etc., but you know who you love today and you love your granddad! I can hear the excitement in your voice. Ohhh, I hope you have a great day! I'm looking forward to seeing you tomorrow.

Luv ya, little honey.

Grandma Bea Goode

CHAPTER 64

Who's That Knocking at My Door?

August 27, 2008

Hi Little Ellie,

You, Mommy, Roxy, and I went shopping today. We all came back to my house for lunch. It was fun! When it was time to go home, you didn't want to leave, so I suggested you stay with me for a while, and then I would drive you home before supper.

We played with the pirate sandbox. We had a tea party in the kitchen. Then we went to the basement and played swinging vines on my curtains. We spent extra time jumping on my bed. Then we settled down to watch *The Jungle Book*. You were very affectionate today, and I was loving it. We sat side by side on the couch, and every once in a while you would rub my arm or lay your head on my shoulder. Awwwww.

Halfway through the movie, you told me you heard a knock on the door. You thought it might be one of your friends. It could be Stewart Little, Mr. Mistoffelees... or Bagheera.

But noooooo, it was Scooby-Doo and Shaggy. We had to go upstairs to check the door. But we were just not fast enough! You told me it was a tough break for us because they didn't wait. When we got to the door they were gone!

We consoled ourselves by driving down to see the cats at Pet Save. Unfortunately, the doors were locked, but we got to watch the cats through the glass. We could see fifteen or twenty of them. One little cat kept pressing himself against the glass, thinking we could scratch him, and when we couldn't, he'd hiss at us. It made us laugh!

Great day! You bring me such joy, little Ellie. I haven't had so much fun since I was a kid myself. (What am I saying? I'm still a kid myself!)

Luv ya, little honey.

Grandma Bea Goode

CHAPTER 65

You Can Read Me Two Stories

September 3, 2008

Hi Little Ellie,

I have been away in Edmonton visiting my family. It was fun, but it is great to be back. I missed my girls. You were glad to see me... after your television show was over. I got lots of hugs and kisses. You loved your shaker rock I had brought back for you. I asked if I could read you your bedtime story. "Yessssss," you said. "Gwandma, you can read me two stories." I was delighted and could hardly wait. "Gwandma," you continued, "you can even feed me rolled oats."

Mommy laughed, "She doesn't even eat rolled oats any more, but if she wants you to feed her, go ahead." I felt so honoured.

We had a fun evening. I got to give you your bath. We played with your little doll. We gave her a bath in her very own tub: an old margarine container. You showed Auntie Sarah and me how you could wet your hair. You had a deep tub tonight, lots of water and lots of fun.

After your bath, Mommy was still trying to settle Roxy, so you and I cuddled in the big chair. I fed you rolled oats. Then Roxy settled and fell asleep. The house fell quiet. You got up from our chair and went over to Mommy. "You read me my stories, okay, Mommy?"

Mommy laughed, "What is wrong, little Ellie? Are you feeling a little mushy tonight?"

"Yesssss," you replied. I wondered if you were going to remember that I was supposed to read you your bedtime stories. "Tomorrow night, you can read me two stories, okay, Gwandma?"

"Okay, little honey."

It felt very peaceful, the way a house can feel when there is a baby sleeping in the bedroom and a delightful tiny girl waiting to hear her bedtime story.

You are such a doll, a real little diplomat, and I smiled all the way home.

Luv ya, little honey.

Grandma Bea Goode

CHAPTER 66

What Happened to Your Hair?

October 16, 2008

Hi Little Ellie,

I was at your place tonight as I usually am when Daddy is on evening shift. You had been to nursery school today, and you were very tired. You had been playing and running with your little friend Blake. You told me you have three other friends, but you don't know their names.

Tonight you were not hungry and didn't want to eat your supper. Mommy spent a lot of time with you because you really didn't seem to be feeling well. You had a long nap, from 3:30 p.m. until 5:00 p.m., and you woke up like a prickly bear. So you and Mommy lay down on the bed and read for a while. Pretty soon you were up, running, and happy again. I tried to feed you rolled oats because you didn't eat any supper. My oh my, the explanation for not eating rolled oats was very involved, but it came down to you were just not hungry tonight and your tummy didn't want anything to eat, especially not rolled oats.

I think that when you spend the day at nursery school, Roxy really misses you. While you were sleeping on the couch, she kept coming over to see if you were awake. When she realized that you were still sleeping, she would pat you on the back and say, "Awwwww." It was like she knew you weren't feeling well. And when you finally shook the sleep off, you spent time with her. "I love my baby sister," you said while trying to hug her (which she objects to) and pick her up (which Mommy objects to.)

As the night moved on, you seemed to have a lot more energy. You were easily distracted and, as usual, easily able to entertain yourself. You quickly slipped into pretend mode. Tonight you were pretending to be a robot with robot motions. "Look what I can do!" you said as you moved your arms stiffly, jumped on one leg, and danced. What a robot! Roxy joined in, and soon everybody was dancing robot style.

Despite some of your get-along moments, you and Roxy are true sisters and not always so loving and cooperative. Last night you were trying to play with your mouse family in your big dollhouse. Roxy was insisting on playing with your mice too. She was being disruptive and was continuously getting in your way. "She's really being a pain tonight, isn't she, Ellie?" said Mommy. "Oh," you replied, "she's even worse than that. She's... she's... she's horrendous!" Mommy and I smiled and tried to keep Roxy away from you for a while.

As bedtime came closer, you sought me out and didn't object when I picked you up for a cuddle. You were tired again, and I started to think that you really weren't feeling well. Mommy put Roxy to bed while you and I played on the couch. Soon you wanted to cuddle. You put your arms around my neck and twirled my hair into tight little spirals as you and I watched television. When Mommy came out of Roxy's room, she took one look at me and began to laugh. "What happened to your hair? Oh, I know, you were lying with Ellie and she was trying to turn you into a mop." This made you laugh and soon we were all giggling.

Later you let me read you a story, which is a big deal for you. You usually want Mommy to read all the stories. Because Roxy is still so young, she goes to bed first. So she is always read to first. But you love how Mommy always reserves book reading time for you and only you. Tonight you wanted me to read to you. I was honoured. You cuddled in, continued to twirl my hair, and told me that you loved me. When the story was over, it was Mommy's time to read. Aren't we lucky? We both got to spend some special time with you.

I felt like I'd been given a gift. My hair might have been twisted into little spirals and my scalp might have felt so tight that I worried it was going to go into a spasm, but my heart felt light and filled with joy, and I smiled all the way home. I am still smiling as I write this.

What a little love you are.

Love ya, honey.

Grandma Bea Goode

CHAPTER 67

You're Not That Smart

December 3, 2008

Hi Little Ellie,

You are such a little doll. You have a real twinkle in your eye that lights up when you are being mischievous and a little dimple in your cheek that stands out when you are being a little devil.

Today, you and Mommy went to the library. When you came back home, you were fidgeting. "Do you need to pee, Ellie?" asked Mommy.

"No!" you said. Fidget, fidget. Mommy took you by the hand and led you to the bathroom and you peed. "Oh," said Mommy, "I'm so smart. Even though you said you didn't need to go pee, I put you on the potty anyway. I just knew you needed to pee. I am so smart!" You jumped off the toilet, walked over to Mommy, put a hand on each side of her face, and said, "Oh, Mommy, you're not that smart." Mommy came out to tell me this and we all had a good chuckle. Your eyes were just dancing. How you love to tease, and how we love it when you do.

I was at your house at bedtime while Mommy was giving you your bath. You were tired and it had been a long day. As you hunkered down into the tub, Mommy and I heard a little voice saying, "There ain't no way I'm going to get my hair washed tonight." Mommy and I looked at each other and burst out laughing. "Ohhhhhkaaaaay," said Mommy. "I guess that's that. Ellie is not getting her hair washed tonight."

After the bath, I grinned at you. "There ain't no way I'm going to watch *The San Diego Zoo* again!" I said. You grinned back. "But, Gwandma, it's my favourite movie!" So of course, we watched *The San Diego Zoo*—again.

I'm always humbled and grateful for cuddle time at the end of the day... and tonight was no exception. My heart swelled, and I am filled with love for you. "Do you want some rolled oats, Ellie, and can I feed you?"

"Yes," you said. Then you teased me. "But it's not rolled oats, Gwandma. It's oatmeal." You laughed, your little dimple winking at me, and cuddled in closer. So tonight I have the great honour of feeding you rolled oats—er, oatmeal. We sat quietly, sometimes holding hands, sometimes not. Either way we were both content.

You make my day.

Love you, little miss "you're not that smart."

Grandma Bea Goode

CHAPTER 68

Mr. Macavity is Vewy, Vewy Scawy

July 3, 2008

Hi Little Ellie,

I haven't written for a while, but I've been thinking about you. The words of the song "Every time I see your picture I smile" keep running through my head.

Last week we had our very first sleepover. I was so excited. We had planned our special day for Friday, but on Thursday night, while I was at your house eating supper, you asked if you could come to my house for a sleepover once we were finished eating. I guess you were excited too. So we packed up and headed to my house. Our first stop was at Tim Horton's for a doughnut: plain with sparkles for you and plain with sugar for me. They had no sparkles, so you and I traded favourites, and you were very pleased.

It was beautiful outside. We spent time out on the sundeck playing ball and blowing bubbles. You sure are fun. I have a new bubble maker that makes hundreds of bubbles easily. I operated the bubble maker while you screamed for joy trying to catch them in the air.

Next it was bath time. We took all the plastic critters and toys from upstairs and brought them down to the tub (my bathroom and bedroom are in the basement). You loved it. Auntie Sarah phoned while you were bathing and you wanted to close the curtain to the tub. It is like a tent in there, and you *love* tents. I was a little uncomfortable with this arrangement, as I couldn't see you, but you reassured me, "I'm okay, Gwandma!"

Afterwards, you stepped out of the tub into your warmed-up-in-the-dryer towel, and we cuddled for a while before getting dressed for bed. I was a little nervous about bedtime (because the last time, you started to feel homesick around this time), but you were totally comfortable.

We watched The Wiggles on TV and then it was time for bed. I read you four stories until you finally exclaimed, "No more stories, Gwandma!"

"Okay, little honey." We held hands, lay quietly, and then... you started to talk about the Broadway movie *Cats*. "I'm not Elliott Jane, Gwandma. I'm Grizabella."

"Okay," I said.

"Grizabella is scared of Mr. Macavity! Vewy, vewy scared. He has flashy eyes! And puffed-up fur. Grizabella dies you know. She goes up to heaven on a rubber tube."

"Does she, honey?" I asked.

"Yessssss," you said, "it is vewy, vewy sad."

"Did you cry, honey?"

"Yesssss," you said. And we lay quietly for a while longer. "It's okay though," you continued. "Grizabella is happy up there."

"Ahhh," I replied.

"Mr. Deuteronomy is scared of Macavity too. Macavity is vewy scawy. Two Jellicle cats come out and he scares them. They hide." This grandmother began to wonder if this was good conversation to have before going to sleep. But you love to talk and you love *Cats*. I promised myself that I would watch the movie with you so that I can understand and have more to offer in our next conversation.

Soon you became very quiet, and when I looked over, you were fast asleep. My goodness, I couldn't believe it. You slept until morning and woke up around 7:00 a.m. But you are a child after your own grandma's heart, and you wanted to stay in bed and snuggle in the early hours of the morning. I loved it.

Soon we were up and eating oatmeal while watching *The Jungle Book*.

We went upstairs to play as we waited for Mommy and baby Roxy to come and take you home.

What a wonderful night—our first sleepover. You are good company, a joy to be with.

I love you, little honey, little Elliott Jane, Grandma's little Jellicle cat!

Grandma Bea Goode

CHAPTER 69

In the United States They Call It Red

July 20, 2008

Hi Little Ellie,

On Friday, Mommy and I took you and Roxy shopping. While riding in the car, Mommy and I discussed the stories that I write for you and Roxy. I told her about some of my spelling problems. For example, in Canada, we spell colour as c-o-l-o-u-r, and in the United States they spell it c-o-l-o-r. I went on to say the same thing about "favour" being spelled f-a-v-o-u-r in Canada and f-a-v-o-r in the United States. I explained how, sometimes, I can get mixed up.

We had a lot of fun shopping. We went to the food court for lunch. You saw a woman eating a soft ice-cream cone, so you wanted to try one... and we did. Mmmmm. I bought you a set of Crayola pencils for when we got home. We rode in the kids' cars and the helicopter ("Come on in, Gwandma." I gave it my best shot!), while Mommy and Roxy went off to do more shopping.

Afterwards, you and I waited while Mommy and Roxy went to buy a few groceries. We played with the colouring pencils. You made lists (your favourite thing to do) and I drew pictures. "What colour pencil did I give you, Ellie?" I asked. You answered with, "I don't know, Gwandma, but in the United States, they call it red!"

You are such a doll, and I love my little colour specialist with all my heart.

Grandma Bea Goode

CHAPTER 70

The Halloween Trick

March 3, 2009

Hi Little Ellie,

We have been spending a lot of time together. Sometimes I get you all to myself.

Mondays and Fridays are our special days, and we both get excited. This Monday, while visiting my house, you spotted some old Halloween treats in a box that I had forgotten about. At the end of our day, you told me, "I am going to take some candy treats home, Gwandma!"

"Are you, little honey?" I replied.

"Yesssss," you said. "I am going to make a pile of treats for Daddy. I am going to trick him."

"You are?" said I.

"Yesssss," you conspired, "when Daddy looks at the pile of treats, he's going to think it's Halloween!"

You and I howled at this. We thought it was the greatest trick in the world.

At suppertime, we went back to your house. When Daddy is working, I often go to your house to help with supper, laundry, and dishes. You'd be surprised at how big of a mess two little girls can make. But tonight, I decided not to do so much. Instead I stayed near you. "I'm tired, Gwandma," you said. You had a bad cold and it was dragging you down. Mommy's hands were full tonight with you feeling under the weather and Roxy so determined to climb, climb, climb. You were looking for attention from Mommy. While the two of you were sitting in the big chair, chilling, and watching TV, Roxy insisted on climbing up beside you. "Mommy," you said, "Roxy kicked me."

"She didn't mean to, Ellie," said Mommy.

"Mommy," you said, "today Roxy bugged me twenty-four times?"

"Is that in one week?" asked Mommy.

"Yesssss," you confirmed.

"Well, it could be worse," teased Mommy. "It could have been twenty-four times in one day!" Mommy grinned at you. You grinned back. We all started to laugh. You have a great sense of humour.

Mommy put Roxy to bed while you and I chilled out. "I'm tired, Gwandma," you said more than once. Awww... I fixed you a pillow and a warm blanket. We sat and watched TV. You twirled my hair into little corkscrews. "I love you, Gwandma."

I love you too, Ellie.

My cup runneth over.

Grandma Bea Goode

CHAPTER 71

I Have a New Friend, Alligator

March 11, 2009

Hi Little Ellie,

Yesterday was Daddy's birthday. How you love a party! You and Grammie D made Daddy a cake with lots of M&M's on top. You looked as pretty as a princess all dressed up for the party in a green chord pantsuit. I giggled to myself when I saw you because your outfit was the opposite of some of your dance outfit creations. Your favourite dancing attire is an old hockey shirt that has a silky feel. It is long and easily becomes a dancing dress.

Speaking about dancing, as Daddy opened his gifts, you grabbed the wrapping paper and organized a dance floor. You are very good at organizing. You made us all laugh (Daddy, Mommy, Granddad, Grammie D, and me.) Then you organized the music tunes to play on your Winnie-the-Pooh radio. You grabbed Roxy by the hand, and the two of you danced like no one was watching—like the wind, without inhibition and with absolute joy. Gosh, you're fun!

Yesterday you went to day care. Mommy and I were worried about this because you are a real homebody. But today you could hardly wait to get there. "I'm going to day care, Gwandma, and I have lots of friends there!"

When you got home from day care, you were still excited. I could hardly wait to hear about your friends. "Do you have a friend at day care, Ellie?" I asked.

"Yesssss," you said. "My friend's name is Tiger, Tiger Tail—no... Tiger Fur, no, Tiger Stripe. He's big. He roars." Just then, Roxy heard the word "roar," and she began to roar at us. (Roxy does not like to talk. She only likes roaring and saying the word "bye.") You and I looked at each other and smiled. "He's not scary though. He helps us," you continued.

"Do you have another friend there?" I asked, hoping to hear of a little girl or boy. "Mommy told me you have lots of friends at day care, like Daniela, Pamela, Gabrielle, Blake, etc."

"Well," you said, "I have a new friend, Alligator, and Swiper is my friend." I laughed. You are very private sometimes. I respect that. And as a friend who respects you, I knew I should stop asking questions. So I did. I just chilled out and enjoyed your company, grateful to learn about whomever you are currently befriending.

How I love you, little honey... and how you make me smile.

Please say hello to Alligator when you get a chance,

Grandma Bea Goode

CHAPTER 72

Just Move in, Gwandma

March 21, 2009

Hi Little Ellie,

I got to spend some time with you yesterday. You were sick again... and so glad to see me. I felt special. Mommy had started you on antibiotics, and already you were feeling a little better... which made me feel better too. Funny how that works.

Tonight, because of your improving health, supper was a celebration. We had a picnic in front of the TV on your Winnie-the-Pooh table and chairs. How you laughed at me as I tried to sit down on the tiny stool, way down, with my knees bent up to my chin. Your laugh started to dwindle, and I could see the wheels of your mind changing tracks. You became very serious. "Could you just move in here with me, Gwandma? You could sleep in my bed. Daddy would wuv it."

"I'm sure he would, little love," I said, "but I think it might be a little crowded."

"Well," you said, "could you just have a sleepover then?"

I was tempted.

Gosh, you fill my heart. In this big, often difficult world, you want me to be your sleepover pal. How cool is that?

We had a really good night. You showed Mommy and me your dance. It is a cross between the Highland Fling and the ballet. Whatever it was, you were in the moment and enjoying your dance enormously... and I was enjoying you.

Tonight, as usual, you had some oatmeal before bed. As you were eating, you asked me if I ever leave the fridge door open. "Not often," I replied.

"Because," you said, "if you leave the fridge door open you will use too much electricity."

"Is that so?" I asked.

"Yesssss," you replied.

"Hmmm," I said. You're a smart little girl.

Before going to bed, you found a little yellow flashlight. "I'm going to take this to bed with me, Gwandma, just in case my night light goes out."

"What a good idea!" I replied.

We cuddled until it was time for Mommy to tuck you in. She'd been looking forward to this all day. So I tucked both of my girls in for the night and left your quiet house with a light heart and a smile as big as the moon.

Good night, little love.

Grandma Bea Goode

About the Author

As a child, Grandma Bea Goode struggled with both writing and spelling but persevered to finish postsecondary schooling and become a secretary. In her early thirties, she decided to return to school in order to become a nurse. She worked at the local hospital for twenty-five years, concluding her time there as the head nurse of the psychiatric floor.

Once retired, she focused her energy on helping to raise her grandchildren. It was after receiving a journal from her daughter that she began to write about the fascinating adventures she would have with Ellie and, later, Roxy. Sharing these stories with those closest to her, there was such an overwhelming response that she decided to publish a select few in hopes of spreading that joy to others.

She is an active member of Toastmasters and the United Church and a passionate volunteer in palliative care.

She continues to write and present her stories wherever she can, making sure that she still has time to partake in whatever adventure her grandchildren create.